Liminal Sermons

Liminal Sermons

ESSAYS WORTH LIVING

ERROL NARAIN

ARPress
45 Dan Road Suite 5
Canton MA 02021

Hotline: 1(888) 821-0229
Fax: 1(508) 545-7580

Ordering Information:
Quantity sales. Special discounts are available on quantity purchases by corporations, associations, and others. For details, contact the publisher at the address above.

Printed in the United States of America.

ISBN-13:   Paperback   979-8-89356-597-3
            Hardcover   979-8-89356-598-0
            eBook   979-8-89356-599-7

Library of Congress Control Number: 2024902788

*Our beliefs bind us to ourselves and
our communities and blind us to the truth*
–Unknown

Jesus was born, lived, and died. The rest is imagination
– Nietzsche

*We worshiped Jesus instead of following him on the same path.
We made Jesus into a mere religion instead of a journey
toward union with God and everything else
This shift made us into a faith of "belonging
and believing" instead of transformation.*
– Richard Rohr

*The aim is to restore the real Jesus to his proper
centrality in the Christian faith and to focus on the man
and his message rather than on doctrines about him*
– Don Cupitt

TABLE OF CONTENTS

DEDICATION

Dedicated to Bishop Ross Cuthbertson, my children Julia, David, Christopher, and grandchildren Naiya, Matthew, Taryn, Samiah, and Meera.

ACKNOWLEDGMENTS

The mysterious God whom all mystics know well has materially and spiritually blessed my life. This God who dwells in all the orders of creation cannot be fully understood or represented in human thought, form, or name.

God, who is not merely a theoretical concept, continues to grace the lives of my ancestral predecessors. They have passed entirely into God's presence in this world. So likewise, without any religious supplication, this same God continues to grace the lives of all, especially family, friends, and associates. The proof of this grace is their witness of love to me, a sustaining guiding light and motivating, humbling influence in my life.

Success in life depends on loving support from those close to you. I will always be grateful to my immediate family - my amazing wife Louisa, Julia, David, Christopher, and our grandchildren Naiya, Matthew, Taryn, Samiah, and Meera. Our grandchildren are a source of hope, delight, and fantastic creativity. May the transforming, energizing, and creative spirit lead them:

Where the mind is without fear
And the head is held high,
Where knowledge is free
Where the world is not broken up into
fragments by narrow domestic walls,
and where words come out from the depth of truth.

My gratitude extends to many teachers whose works have been answers to prayer. I came across their books, videos, etc., at the most needed time when troubling questions propelled me into liminal space, desperately seeking answers. So many luminary persons have helped, especially Richard Rohr, Phyllis Tickle, Brian McLaren, Don Cupitt, Sir David Hawkins, Jeremy Griffith, Bart D. Ehrman, Neil deGrasse Tyson, James W. Fowler, David Eagleman, Harvey Fox, Arundhati Roy, Bishop Shelby Spong, Anand Giridharadas, Krista Tippett, Slavoj Zizek, Cornel West, Noam Chomsky, Vandana Shiva, Michael Brooks, et al.

Thank you to my grandchildren Taryn Rooks and Samiah Narain, for your artwork on the front and back covers. They respectively depict liminal space, the twilight hours of every natural day.

INTRODUCTION

Early in his marriage, my older son surprised me when he shared that he had decided not to belong to my Church nor attend my church services. At this time, I was a seasoned senior priest in the Episcopal/Anglican church in the USA, which I served for more than 30 years. In my previous assignment, I served in South Africa until my exile in 1987, the peak of the apartheid era clampdown on all individual activists and organizations for social change.

The day my son informed me of his decision to distance himself from the Church, I was not defensive. Nor was I offended, disappointed, or shocked that my flesh and blood had decided to turn his back on institutional religion. Instead, at that moment, I realized that Jesus also made the same decision to distance himself from religion that had become a toxic institution.

My son explained that he had taken a class in Biblical Studies at College. For centuries changes in science, historical thinking, and philosophy had eroded cherished beliefs. However, my son's teacher had succeeded in dissolving all traditional dogmas in my son's mind leading him to the wisdom of a critical mind and faith.

I still remember my son's words to me on that day. He said he was tired of hearing the same humdrum, uncorroborated messages presented as facts. In a sentence, my son had concisely communicated that the institutional Church, its programs, and worship had failed dismally in helping its constituents in *their* crucial questions. So I began to ask questions about the Church, God, Jesus, the Bible, doctrines, spirituality, and the Church's role in this world. My son had turned me in a new direction of spirituality for knowledge, wisdom, faith, and existential meaning in this world.

My son was not alone, in his opinion. So many new Evangelicals like Brian McLaren, Tony Jones, Peter Rollins, Episcopalians like Bishop Michael Curry, Phyllis Tickle, Diana Butler Bass, Lutherans like Nadia-Bolz Weber, and a groundswell of others in other faith traditions emerged to question dogmatic, theoretical religion in the context of the new world of science, critical thinking, the expanding universe and the present Age of Information.

The institutional Church machine had turned out many mature adults who say they are spiritual but not religious. Then, the pendulum had swung back in history to open talk of God is Dead and religionless Christianity. Today, seekers are looking for a church beyond doctrines, dogma, and beliefs. Diana Butler Bass talks about the need for Christianity after religion.

Many seek answers in the mystic wisdom tradition, a suppressed phenomenon in all legalistic faith traditions. Meister Eckhart, Theresa of Avila, Catherine of Siena, Julian of Norwich, Rudolf Otto, and Rumi were mystics in the West. In the 5th Century, mystics in the early Church retreated from the institutionalizing imperial tendency to the desert places in the Empire. They feared the loss of their souls if they remained.

In the 1900s, there was a Protestant Reformation in the USA. These American Protestants feared the historical-critical approach to the Bible threatened its unscientific worldview, unsuspecting mind, and supernatural beliefs. The Protestant Reformation, in its conferences, to stop the threat adopted a set of non-negotiable fundamental beliefs necessary for salvation. The American reformation succeeded in raising the Bible's authority to absolute truth in all life matters. The man, Jesus of Nazareth, was made into God, supplanting the work of God as Christ, the spirit in history. For the believer, the theory of atonement by the blood sacrifice of Jesus was effective for purification, sanctification, redemption, and salvation.

Fundamentalism's belief in the sole authority of the scriptures continues to be the primary stumbling block to progress in the world, the Elephant in the room of all Christendom. The Bible approached from this perspective supports the divisive, corrupt, dysfunctional human condition.

An alternate approach to conceptual religion and the sacred scriptures is necessary for the salvation of the Church and personal spiritual growth. Harvey Cox. Hollis Research, Professor of Divinity at Harvard, sees this era as the rise and fall of belief and the coming age of the spirit. In addition, we have seen the phenomenon of the *nones*, those of no religious affiliation seeking direct encounter, and spiritual oneness with God beyond theoretical faith. Don Cupitt laments that dogmatic religion adapts Christianity to fit culture to the establishment's demands and not the people's demands.

Readers of the Bible, traditional evangelical students, read back the institution's dogmas as exegesis into the original metaphors of the New Testament. Instead, present wisdom advises starting first from Jesus himself in the synoptic gospels of Mark, Matthew, and Luke for authentic faith. Jesus, the man, and his message must be the focus- not the egoist doctrines about him.

The secret way of Jesus included the loss of the self, the dying of the Ego/Self, and unconditional Love for God and neighbor. The opposite of fear is love. Ego fears love. The Ego/Self lives at a place distant from God in a state of apostasy, obsessed with self-survival. To live in a union with love means letting go, the sacrifice of the Ego, and its vain idols. Ironically, the Self/ Ego leads itself to death and new life. The new life is the unconditional Love of God.

Sufi mystics focus on generous living. In the Sufi dance, the twirling of life propels one into the place where one receives from God to give to others. Suffering, loss, illness, pandemics, disease, and so on, the dance of life propels us to the liminal, in-between, twilight place of darkness, nothingness, Light, Love, and new life.

Poets, writers, sages, prophets, students, sermon writers, and everyone struggling as saints, see the liminal place as the place of contemplation and creativity. In this place, darkness, trauma, suffering, etc., serves as the teacher. In this place, immense resources for creativity, hope, and transformation await the visitor. God heals in darkness. Jesus called this place the Kingdom of God in this world.

In the twilight place, darkness is a place of resurrection, as the following poem confirms:

LIMINAL

Early they rose
To be in the place
Where night salutes the dawn
Where angels bear,
And sages hear
Words from the heart of Good
Early they ran
To the place of Dark
Where death dissolves into life

Angels they saw
And with awe
Bursting to tell of new life
Early we rise
To the conscious State within
Where self counsels with God
Eager to unlearn and learn
Willing to burn
With God for the Love of the World

All the greats, like Jesus, prefer to live in this state of permanent liminality. Richard Rohr describes this lifestyle as being silent, not speaking, empty, not complete, not the persona but anonymity, broke, yet plenty. Life is a constant pattern of trusted patterns, personal relationships, and the illusion of fragmentation. Trauma propels one into a liminal space where the small self finds the perspective of the Great and the bigger self of love.

The following poem dissects the permanent mystic lifestyle into a moment, the moment of contemplative, authentic prayer. The first stanza reflects Ego and egoist religion's vain response to personal sickness and hysteria in the dysfunctional human condition. Ego's non-existent God appears distant, numb, and powerless, no more than a concept, an idea, a belief. The second stanza is what we already know and experience in life- mysterious solidarity, African *ubuntu,* the fullness of the presence of God's goodness in others, other creatures, and the natural world. The Ego holds the mind captive, almost succeeding in stopping the flow of love from the heart, God's constant presence, the love-beat in the world. Jesus in Christ calls us to the life lived in a liminal space where this love and mercy are abundant in this world. The liminal space is the in-between place, the constant dynamic relationship of death, resurrection, and enlightenment.

THIS WORLD IS MY HOME
Emmanuel, God is with Us

Praying to God
A concept, a thought, an idea, a belief
Sequestered in Heaven
In an alternate universe,
Practicing social distancing.
In fear of the virus of Sin
No eyes to see the tears, no heart to feel the pain,
no arms to embrace with compassion
Deaf to the cries of Christ embodied in the tragic
The Beloved Who cry
Where are you? Why have you forsaken us?

Come to me all ye who worry and labor
Seek, and ye will find
When you look into the eyes of someone else
You will see the face of God
Turn to me within you
Look for me in every place
I am within you. I am among you.
I am in this world
This world is my home, my Heaven.
Join me in the dance of love

In Christianity, death and resurrection are two sides of the same coin. One lets go of lonely, isolated existence for the sake of a deeper union with God, the Cosmos, and the community. The soul thrives on suffering, while Ego/Self thrives on painless success for self-survival. The soul, the bigger self in God, seeks purpose, meaning, and hope to flourish. Mystic hope is not an optimistic feeling. Mystic hope draws from the source within, even in unfavorable circumstances.

The Christian message in the sacred scriptures centers on direct access of immediate grace for wise living and just action. The traditional theories about incarnation and substitutionary atonement theories obscure who Jesus was and his saving message. Don Cupitt advises reexamination of the conventional doctrine to discover Jesus and know his way. Cupitt says this work aims to restore the historical Jesus to his proper centrality in the Christian faith as a man. Also, the focus will be on the man and his message rather than on doctrines about him. Nietzsche cynically spoke the truth when he remarked that Jesus was born, lived, died, and the rest is imagination. The theories of atonement, payment for sins, and substitution developed as doctrines over 200 years. Today, believers read these doctrines into the New Testament. Jesus only taught the mystic way for union with the God of transformative Love. This God is not an angry, punitive God who dispenses retributive justice.

Sages in the Hebrew Bible explained faith in living relational terms- just and fair personal relationships with God and others. God's prophets often labeled God's people as playing the whore. Jesus balked on the religious definition of faith- strict adherence to legalistic religion. Instead, Jesus invited people into oneness with the God of Love in the Kingdom at hand. There is no division, bigotry, dualism, binary thinking, violence, or competition in God's Kingdom at hand, the liminal space, except contemplation of the God who is unconditional love. The Kingdom is the place where the Ego as the "I" dissolves into the "We" and "Us." In John's gospel, Jesus, the High Priest, prays for solidarity and that all may be one as he(Jesus) and God are one.

Prophets and sages, old and new, proclaim that religion by itself is humanistic. God cannot be a belief but an experience. For the present, the traditional doctrine of biblicism and theology grounded on speculative assumptions must make way for the God present in creation. God's spirit, the Christ, is calling for a new reformation for transformation. Global Capitalism, natural tsunamis, pandemics of war, natural disasters, and viruses point to the faultlines in the Church, the state, and the human condition. The times are urgent. The anguished cries of the suffering moan from the abyss of the Dark. The questioning prayers of the anxious people echo in the hollow chamber of man's Ziggurat construction of high-stacked beliefs that go nowhere.

This book of sermonic essays responds to questions raised by those I minister to in South Africa, the USA, and other parts of the world. The answers come from that liminal dark place of death and resurrection/ awakening/ enlightenment. I hope these essays will enlighten your path as a pilgrim, stimulate the mind, quicken the heart, and strengthen the soul for unconditional love in this world.

ONE

Death is the way of every person. How can we understand
and talk about death without being morbid? Does death have
the answer to the riddle about grief and life in general?

Dust we are, and unto God, we return

The ritual of the imposition of ashes to signify Lent's start, a period of fasting in the catholic Christian tradition on Ash Wednesday, includes the sobering and discomforting words of the title above. These words come from Genesis 3:19: *Remember that dust you are, and unto dust, you shall return.* Genesis, the Hebrew and Christian Bible's first book, contains the prescient, ahistorical, mythical narrative of the planet's creation. This creation story includes creating the first spiritual human called Adam from dust. The process of human creation ends with God breathing life into Adam's nostrils. The catholic Christian tradition uses these solemn words reminding all humans of their mortality, the physical body's beginning, and the return of the body-dust initially borrowed from the earth. Life in God's spirit continues after sowing the physical body, including the brain, in the ground. Finally, the spirit body and consciousness attain unitive consciousness with the God of unconditional love.

For the spiritual-inclined- mystics like Jesus, Paul, and a host of others like Francis of Assisi, death and dying are integral to the paradox of life, two sides of the same coin. Mystics enjoy the gifts of abundant, transformative life through being in God, the spiritual practices of sacrifice, dying, denial, detachment, loss, and eventually death of the two physical bodies, namely body and mind. Jesus taught this secret wise way of living in the parable of the heavily laden camel struggling through the small side gate in the city wall, called the "eye of the needle." This parable explains the mystic's practical way of life by continually letting go of flawed egoist cultural discriminatory accretions and dying to selfish and self-serving aspirations. Nevertheless, one can still experience the new way of transforming being through loss and death long before one dies. This life Jesus identified as the eternal newness of life, the transformed life lived in union with God, who is spirit. The *Peace Prayer* attributed to St. Francis of Assisi concisely summarizes this abundant fulfilled living before physical death: *In dying, we are born to eternal life.*

What must be "let go?" What must one put to death in our mortal bodies? What must one leave behind? The Book of Genesis account of creation is not a science record of observations and proofs, nor a historical factual record of events. Still, the book contains symbolic paradigms for understanding, meaning, and purpose for living. The Hebrew and Christian Bible is believable in its storytelling of creating the planet and its living creatures. First, there existed the nameless universal, primordial spirit without gender and anthropomorphic considerations. This God-spirit breathes its life-giving spirit into the dust-created structure, making the first human a living soul.

In the Christian Bible, John in his gospel, and Paul in the Colossian letter, identifies this Godly spirit as the Christ, the universal spirit that births the Cosmos and dwells in all living creatures. In John's gospel, the mythical event of creating humans in Genesis repeats in the birth-event of Jesus of Nazareth. John points out this event was not a singularly once-off unique moment in the birth of Jesus of Nazareth. Before and after Jesus, born of fleshly mothers, everyone is animated and enlightened by the universal Christ. The creation event in Genesis declares that every human birth is an incarnation of the pre-existent ubiquitous Christ before space and time. Every human and all creation bear God's stamp of God's likeness and image. Humans have a physical body and mind and a spiritual body that houses the universal God in Christ.

The Biblical record of creation in Genesis 1-11 does not differ significantly from modern Science's evolutionary account of sequential events. The Bible and Science tell similar stories of the elemental human make-up and the place of humans in the order of creation. Science affirms that 13.8 billion years ago, planets formed after the atomic explosion of a supernova called the Big Bang. The earth's age is 4.5 billion years, and microscopic human life began in a primordial soup 3.5 billion years ago. Every living species, about 500 documented species, has a common ancestor. The first human ancestors appeared between 5 million and 7 million years ago. The modern human is a young species on the planet, a late-comer- some 300,000-250,000 years ago. The Genesis1-11 segment accounts for the rise of consciousness and the Ego, individualistic pride, the accumulating and competitive spirit, and the crowning mental creation of civilization's vanity.

The primate's brain volume, a marvelous, sophisticated machine of interconnected dynamic energy and neurons, has tripled in body size over the last 3 million years, especially between 800,000 and 200,000 years. The large modern human brain size of 2.5 lbs., capable of processing new and enormous information, served as a significant advantage during climate and planet change caused by tectonic shifts. The brain enlarged to cope with increasing social competition, developing survival responses as food resources dwindled. Human competition, selfishness, and aggression are now instinctual genetic behaviors that dominate the human psychotic mind, sustaining the corrupt, dysfunctional social condition. In their genes, humans have the legacy of conduct derived from the lower biological species and groups- fish, reptiles, amphibia, and primates. When the situation demands, humans react instinctively like the earlier species in the evolutionary ladder. As the brain developed and increased in size, humans also gained the ability to use denial as a coping mechanism. Denial is a strategy that all individuals have to learn to survive in group living. The animalistic behavior of competition, selfishness, aggression, and human denial in the corrupt human condition, contributes to the perplexing problem of depression and suicide in human society and social dysfunction. The world presents us with the judgmentally harsh truth that our conscious developed mind wrecked paradise and separates individuals from the universal spirit's goodness- and primordial human nature, the Christ. Our most significant problem and suffering arise from human memory loss of one's divine nature and mental bondage to our necessary earthen physical bodies' base desires and needs.

Modern Science has revealed a tremendous power available in the universe for human progress, enjoyment, and the noble pursuit of life. Scientists have confirmed that the Cosmos comprises a physical structure called Dark Matter, yet not fully observed, therefore not wholly understood. Palpable energy or spirit exists in space where matter dies, disappears into "dark holes," and resurrects in glorious new bodies better adapted for survival and living.

The human structure comprises three bodies- two material bodies, including the brain with its mental ability- and the third body, the spiritual body. At the time of death, the physical body- body, and mind- returns to the dust, the place from when it came. When humans die, they pay back the debt of dust borrowed from the ground, cell by cell, atom by atom. The physical bodies do not go further from the planet from which they came. Humans are much of what they eat. The spirit energy body, the non-physical, goes back to join with the Dark Matter of energy in space. Death, a great blessing, frees the human body from its entrapment to the whims of the physical mind and body, the egoist life of survival, and the busyness of constant, joyless sowing and reaping in the fields of the corrupt human condition. In the Christian doctrinal burial rite, the body sown to the earth makes its return to the ground from whence it came. The spirit body rises to join its source, the spirit in the universe. Dark Energy or God in the Cosmos adjusts, welcomes, and accommodates the arrival of all who die. The scriptural metaphor expresses this meaning in the *heavenly host rejoicing to receive the sinful dead separated from God's presence.*

In this life, before death, our physical and psychological, mental bodies possess limited data. This limited data is insufficient, unable to help us escape life's trap, set by ourselves and others. Our egoist persona provides the illusion of individuality, separation from God, and a false sense of independence and security. Still, Ego imprisons us in our likes and dislikes. Only a sense of balance between the spirit body's physical bodies and spirit can free one from this egoist mental trap. Freedom without equilibrium leads to destruction, lack of solidarity, community, and anarchy in life before death. Only the experience of Christ, God's presence- the true self within and without, can help free us from Ego's entrapment.

The human species have reached the peak of its physical and mental development. Science has confirmed that even the human brain is shrinking. The answer to the riddle of life on this side of death depends strictly on balanced living between the needs of our physical bodies and the bliss body, the spirit body. The business pursuit of vision, purpose, meaning, and goals is a temporary *efficient* solution in the corrupt human condition. The "civilized" world is fleet and passes away every 500 years. What the human creates is temporary. As the Bible says, the physical human body also has a brief life span, *three-score and ten years.* Should one set vision, goals, and purpose for life? Living is not a human leadership project. Only the highly insane patriots live by goal and purpose. If there is a purpose to live, this purpose is abundant living. Abundant life is living life to its fullest with unlimited, often meaningless exploration, questioning, and dying to know this world in its entirety.

Therefore, life is a paradox of dying and living. In the end, we finally die physically. We rise spiritually to a new life in union with universal spirit and Dark Matter in this Cosmos. The Book of Genesis and other writings from mystics like Paul and John identify that this universal spirit or energy is the Christ of creation for transformation and grace for knowledge and practical wisdom. In Paul's letter to the Corinthians and Colossians, Paul speaks of receiving a new body in the twinkling of an eye at the point of death. His conversion on the Damascus Road is an explanation of this death and rising.

The spirit-body, separated from the physical body, including the mind, mysteriously takes on a new body and mind at life's end. Jesus taught his learners to die, and those who listened will be new beings requiring *new wineskin for the new wine.* Paul does not spell out precisely the nature of this new body. Those who experience spiritual ecstasy, living out of one's body, dying to self, and rising, bring gifts of a new way of being and seeing that characterize life generally. Paul also assured the Ephesian church that humans who die sit with Christ in the heights of heavenly bliss, enjoying an astronaut's view of the planet. Jesus knew this life personally, calling it the Kingdom of God or Heaven, a dynamic place of contemplation, transformation, and grace for union with God and the newness of life. Many cultures believe that when one dies, they become stars in the heavenly Cosmos.

The blissful life, intentional separation from the body-mind physical bodies to merge with the source of bliss in the world, is possible before death. Mystics knew how to live a blissful life. They performed practices that subdued the Ego, suppressed the physical desires for public persona aspirations, wealth, and selfish satisfaction. The mystics described this way as dying to self and rising to a new way of being human in this world. Paul talks about this Jesus experience in his letter to the Philippians. Similarly, Paul understood baptism's ritual as dying with Christ and rising to the new life in Christ.

In death, the physical body and brain return to the ground. The spiritual body attains freedom from imprisonment in the physical body and the egoist mind and attachment to its cultural creations in this world. Release from death brings life in union with Christ and God's justice mission for peace in this world. Those who die do not go too far from the living. The dead do not die but remain in the liminal space. The Irish call liminal space the thin- place where the division between heaven and earth, space and time collapse, and God the universal Christ is present.

For Paul, those in a relationship with Christ live in a mystic state of constant dying, rising, and transformation. The faithful one does not grieve the dead in the fashion of those uninformed and unaware of humans' evolutionary creation, life in God's kingdom, God's tangible presence in creation's design, Jesus's spiritual way of self-emptying, and death to self. The church's burial rite includes the victorious shout at the moment of committal to the ground: *We go down to the ground shouting, Alleluia, Alleluia, Alleluia!*

Jesus taught that few find the way of faith, the portal to the assurance in the life of severe distress, sorrow, loss, and death. Both Jesus and Paul alerted their disciples to the physical body's oppressive power of denial over the spiritual body. Both these prophets warned against unsuccessful false religious practices. Jesus himself avoided organized religion. He only frequented the synagogue and Temple to fulfill his prophetic ministry. Paul established communities of constant contemplative prayer, action, learning, fellowship, and service to those in need. Paul boasted about his ecstatic mystical liminal experiences of reaching the seventh heaven in Kabbalistic tradition. Jesus and Paul never shied away from speaking of death. Paul longed for the day when he could be free from the physical body, the "mortal body," but sternly warned against cowardly suicide. In the Hindu yogic tradition, one can do a sadhana, a spiritual practice to pitch the life intensity to such a high point that life slips out of the physical body altogether. Life also naturally leaves the physical body when the weakened body cannot sustain life.

The physical body feels the pain of loss when death occurs. This loss becomes unbearable if the physical body is unaware of grace in the spiritual body. Suppose one is unaware of the spiritual body and only knows the narrow mental path of beliefs and does not understand death as illusory. In that case, the human physical body is overwhelmed by grief. Others cope with other mental gymnastics of avoidance and denial. The expert Kubler-Ross identifies five stages of grief and loss- anger, denial, bargaining, depression, and acceptance. In the grieving process, one does not walk a straight line of grief from denial to resignation. The stages of grief are merely signs to identify our feelings at a given moment. As grieving humans, we are a dynamic wax ball of often uncontrollable emotions- anger, denial, bargaining, depression, and acceptance- which bombard one all at once. We should not judge a person's grief experiences and expect that they "pull themselves together." Each person's experience is uniquely different. Grief is a process. To those who understand and follow a spiritual path exemplified by Jesus, joy does come in the morning. This result takes intention, time, hard work, knowing the self, spiritual practice, and experiencing the world as abounding in the presence of knowledge for wisdom.

The noblest dreams are born in the liminal space, in the quiet crucible of one's personal and private sufferings, and the most significant gifts are received. God, like gold, is the end product of the destruction of Ego's vain productions in the false self. Grief propels one into the darkness of liminal space, where God's grace breaks down life's trusted patterns of one's lonesome leanings. The resolution of grief's battle is the balanced life and the miracle of the blessing of wholeness and health. Because God is always present in our sufferings, death is an illusion. God's presence turns depression into good depression. In the race of life, death is the baton exchange of life passing into life. God only is life, and God is eternal. The illusion of death is merely a portal, the gateway to abundant living in Christ. This life is heavenly bliss, a present experience before death. Church services memorializing those who die should celebrate homecoming rather than home-going. There is no particular place called heaven, for heaven is where God is. God is everywhere and more significant than the Cosmos. There is no punishment place called hell, for God is unconditional love. The dead do not go far from us. They live in God, and God is here with us.

An appropriate prayer as the physical body is committed to the dust from whence it came:

> ***God on High***
> ***Hear our Prayer***
> ***You've always been there***
> ***Bring them Home.***

TWO

The mystic tradition searches for knowledge, truth, and wisdom in a mysterious, relative, constantly changing world. The search for truth demands a humble, respectful attitude accompanied by praise, awe, and wonder. The world's health depends on mystics, theologians, and scientists joining hands as pilgrims on the one path towards truth.

Mystic, Theologian, Scientist, and the pursuit of Truth

Mystics are ordinary humans asking big questions about life in general. Mystics humbly confess that they do not know everything. They live by the maxim: *I don't know.* The work of scientists provides temporary facts for the mystic. Mystics rely on science for facts and use the open-ended scientific method of inquiry in their work. God for mystics is too big to be contained in a closed system. God and the Cosmos for mystics is a mystery, ever-expanding, and vast. Truth for mystics cannot be reduced to mere rapturous ecstatic feeling and thought. Mystics possess a courageous faith that is critical of finite idolized representations. Paul discouraged idol worship because they failed miserably in conveying the fullness of God's truth and nature. Extremely religious humans tend to exchange the creator God for the creature made with human hands. Idols represent more the creature than God. Nietzsche thinks the idea, the representation of God as a crutch that makes some humans feel secure.

Mystics are ordinary persons intent on disciplining and intensifying the spiritual body's experience of God's spirit and nature to practice compassionate solidarity with others. The mystic way includes spiritual practices that subdue the physical bodies' desires for the experience of ecstasy, that is, the reality beyond and outside of the structural bodies' personal experience. The prophet Mohammed's out-of-body experiences were more rupturing than rapture. Each of his exuberant spiritual experiences could have easily killed him. He spent much time recovering after each spiritual experience. The mystic way is a process that first blows the mind, secondly *bedazzles,* and *thirdly transforms.* Mystics subscribe to faith beyond beliefs understood in relational terms. This relational faith with everything speaks to the wide-eyed intelligence in one. It helps rediscover a religion that raises one to adulthood, and delivers from an immature preservation state as cryogenic embryos. According to Fowler and Maslow, the highest form of mature religion is universal, relational, and solidarity.

Modern scientists also employ the open-ended inquiry method in their work. The path is untidy, strewn with old, new, and fluid answers with limited shelf life. Yet, the inquiry into truth springs forth from an open mind, alert to a vast world, rapidly expanding, changing and naturally pregnant with the reality of the riveting mystery, ambiguities, riddles, and possibilities.

The mystic relationship with this world, its understanding, and its meaning are vital for a deep spirituality and knowledge of God. Cox explains this spirituality as a "move to horizontal transcendence" or "turning to the immanent." He adds that one should speak of spirituality as the rediscovery of the sacred in the immanent, the spiritual within the secular. The metaphysic poet Gerard Manley Hopkins describes this world as being charged with the grandeur of God. The disciples of St. Francis spoke of God as "brother sun" or "sister moon." Both mystic and scientist reverently bow in awe and wonder before the vast mystery and grandeur of this universe.

The mystic faith also avoids an attitude of certainty, exceedingly arrogant confidence in external legalism, which reduces religion to fundamentalist propositional beliefs, dogma, and doctrine. Further, the mystic resists falling into the trap of shrinking God into a noun or pronoun, name, symbols, or person. The mystic, like the scientist, employs suspicion, a questioning and challenging stance, paradoxical explanations of knowing, a holding onto things sensed, and a letting go of flawed information. God, for mystics, is not an "object" of contemplation as Duns Scotus and the philosophical method of Descartes proposed. God is an existential encounter, an immediate sensual experience of the spirit of creation. God is something and [no] thing at the same time, a paradox. Naming God for mystics reduces God to something, a finite cultural comprehension, a creature, an image emanating from the human mind, and in most cases, a mere anthropomorphic conjecture. Rudolf Otto explains this when he says: "God is not, so to speak, wholly 'wholly other.' That aspect of Deity, the mysterious overplus, surpasses all that can be clearly understood and appraised. There should be strong resistance to making God-man and reducing the "Sacred and Holy to the measure of our human reason." Otto's revelation of God is the plus and overplus experience, transcending any language, culture, and religious limitations.

Otto's theology is at the heart of C.S. Lewis's poem *"Footnote to All Prayers."*

> He whom I bow to only knows to whom I bow
> When I attempt the ineffable Name, murmuring Thou,
> And dream of Pheidian fancies and embrace in heart
> Symbols (I know) which cannot be the thing Thou art.
> Thus always, taken at their word, all prayers blaspheme

Worshipping with frail images a folk-lore dream,
And all men in their praying, self-deceived, address
The coinage of their own unquiet thoughts, unless
Thou in magnetic mercy to Thyself divert
Our arrows, aimed unskillfully, beyond desert.
And all men are idolators, crying unheard
To a deaf idol if Thou takes them at their word.
Take not, O Lord, our literal sense. Lord, in thy great
Unbroken speech our limping metaphor translate.

The mystic Meister Eckhart preached against idolizing God by naming and destroying God's oneness of being. In his sermon 72: God is above all names and above nature. In his sermon 11, Meister Eckhart talks of "the peak of the soul not wanting God as Holy Ghost nor the Son. Nor does the soul want God, as he is God. The soul desires a nobler, better thing than God having a name." Even the Christian concept of the Trinity, especially in its literalism, is not above criticism among mystics who see God as wholly "other" and one. The Trinity is a traditional institutional doctrinal conceptualism by committee – not a revelation.

There is a way of getting around the problem of inadequately speaking about and scripting God. The literary tools of stories and poetry convey a partial understanding of God and simultaneously leaves room for the "overplus" that is God. When speaking of God in a mystical experience, we can be comfortable only when appraisal language avoids literalism using the tools of metaphor, paradox, and analogy. This honest way of pursuing the truth, the method of epistemological or intellectual humility, avoids linguistic poverty and hubris when exploring and appraising God, who is the only ultimate Truth and Reality.

The main problem in science and religion today is the human desire for certainty. Voltaire said: "Uncertainty is an uncomfortable position, but certainty is an absurd one." Krista Tippett says to name God is problematic for the precise reason that God is named, using limited and flawed human resources of perception. She explains that humans are *containers* for insights fashioned in the human condition's frailty and passion. Religion for Tippett becomes problematic because of its entanglement with human identity. She says: "There is nothing more intimate and volatile than that, especially in an age of global transition." Religion is the cause of much of the world's division and violence, threatening democracy, and civilization globally. Because religion is a quest for truth, it cannot be a private affair between consenting adults. For Tippett, there must always be a religious [spiritual] voice in public life. It could serve as a voice of balance in extreme competing certainties which have hijacked the cultural discourse. "In the vast middle, faith is about questions and answers. It is possible to be a believer and listener at the same time, to be fervent but searching to honor the truth of one's convictions and the mystery of the convictions of others".

Both mystics and scientists are on the same journey of discovery of truth and meaning for life. For the mystic, the locus of the divine mystery is the same locus for the mystery of the cosmos. Any mystic, theologian, or scientist student of truth must include this universe as a mystery in the ultimate environment's study. In modern religion, this intelligent quest goes beyond a closed, rationalized fundamentalist ideological system. Fundamentalism is the balkanization of our world by using conflicting ideological beliefs and holding captive the true believer's faith. The true disciple (student) chooses the road of explorative learning, discovering the God within and beyond the gods of one's own making, the God beyond all tribal religious belief. Spiritual questions don't go away, nor does a sense of wonder and mystery cease in the absence of an *idea* that is God. The God of ideas is an illusion emanating from the magician's egoist mind, and therefore does not exist.

For the true mystic, theologian, and scientist, the quest for truth presents the same challenges. The discoveries on the journey towards truth using the open-ended system's proven method is the beginning of a never-ending journey. The doctrinal religion's God and the atheist's God is the same God that emanates from the egoist human. Both the believer and atheist argue about the same non-existent God. God is not an idea that emanates from the human mind. No religion possesses the cornerstone on the God who is too vast for one sectarian religion's story. We know too little of this universe to position on the partial understanding of the Universe or partial perception of God, who may not exist.

God is not an idea but an experience that includes and is beyond the single or collective communal thought capacity. Modern Fundamentalism, the reduction of God to a set of ideological beliefs, does a disservice to the quest of God's immanent presence and elusive Truth in this world for its welfare. The modern world calls for a learner who is a mystic-scientist- theologian. The student cannot be lazy or distracted in this crucial endeavor. The scientist, theologian, and mystic practitioner cannot arbitrarily make pit stops the goal of the journey towards truth. The journey is to the very heart of the divine mystery, the quest for the Holy Grail, the beginning of all things. David Eagleman offers the following words to subdue the attitude of certainty. He says: "that living in this strange world; we must strive to live a life free from dogma, full of awe and wonder, celebrating possibility and praising uncertainty." Paul advised: Now I see through a glass dimly, but then I shall see face to face". Like scientists, reasonable theologians must use these words: I don't know when studying the mystery of God and the Cosmos.

THREE

The dysfunctional human condition throws up leaders, well-meaning in their intent. Repeatedly such leadership and their movements have partially succeeded in their purpose to abolish corruption effectively. This sermon looks at the character and work of three leaders, namely, Gandhi, Martin Luther King Jr, and Mandela, in the light of the man Jesus of Nazareth.

There is None Like Jesus. No, Not One

Charles Dickens described the period before the French Revolution as the in-between times. He writes: "*it was the best of times, it was the worst of times, it was the age of wisdom, it was the time of foolishness, it was the epoch of belief, it was the epoch of incredulity, it was the season of Light, it was the season of darkness, it was the spring of hope, it was the winter of despair, we had everything before us, we had nothing before us, we were all going direct to Heaven, we were all going direct the other way- in short, the period was so far like the present period, that some of its noisiest authorities insisted on its being received, for good or for evil, in the superlative degree of comparison only.*" Charles Dickens could have been describing the present era.

Dickens described the perfect storm that drives the spiritually inclined into liminal space, the place of God and contemplative prayer. The Latin root of the word "portal" translates into threshold, edge, or gateway. Liminal space, the location of transition, is where the soul withdraws to seek solace and answers. One cannot rudely force entry past the doorway. There are no boundaries in this dynamic place of waiting between the darkness of the present moment and the dawning Light. At first, the Light that is God hardly noticeable pushes through the gloom of the moment, growing brighter, waiting for the sacred opportune moment to approach. God as the energetic spirit is beyond, infinite, unknowable mystery, yet embedded in the context of the trauma.

God reveals Godself as a concrete reality in these present dark times of police brutality in the USA. Police in public notice routinely strangle Blacks by applying chokeholds or the standard kneeling pressure at the back of the neck for periods lasting more than nine minutes, as in the case of George Floyd. Blacks in the USA, even children younger than toddlers, live in constant fear of police brutality, incarceration, violence, and disenfranchisement within the system of American liberal, capitalist democracy. The concerned God for the welfare of humanity is both infinite, unknowable, a mystery. God faithfully reveals a timely immediate presence as people globally gather to march on the streets to protest for justice before peace.

The USA's present pandemic social and health crises is a double-edged sword, the novel mutating strain of the Coronavirus and the tireless entrenched disease of institutional capitalist racism. Dysfunction in the corrupt social condition raises single charismatic heroes to wage war against evil in high places. In the present era, things have changed. Singular heroes do not run the show. Thousands under organic collective leadership can take to the streets within a digital instant to protest against institutional brutality and other social evils. The hitherto suppressed history of capitalist colonialism is all the more critical to the never-ending struggle for freedom. This national crisis, gone international, has brought the religious and secular establishments to their knees.

On the one hand, the institutional narcissistic Ego seeks disingenuous solutions that will keep its structures intact. On the other hand, the collective prayer of the organic grassroots protest proposes the complete dismantling of the failed American social experiment. What the institution proposes, the grassroots movement disposes. The establishment slogan is for reform, while the struggle's slogan cries out for deform.

The powerful, in their response, treat racism as a mere identity crisis and stubbornly refuse to see the inextricable connection of power to racism. Corporations and their local agencies strongly direct and influence the conversation to solve issues. Their ghostly presence guarantees the decision-making progress and outcome through paid representatives. This typical scenario has already played out in the national struggle against police brutality. The people call for defunding the police department and more significant investment for development in the community. The establishment insists on liberal education programs of its police officers and superficial reform of the law agency. Bureaucracy disingenuously refuses to deal with the primary issue of liberation and empowerment of the people. The institution also deals in the same way when women raise their concerns. The establishment view women and their problems as stemming from an identity crisis and not rooted in the dysfunctional social, political, and economic context. Those in power strongly believe that the solution to social ills depends on reform government.

The religious institution typically issues progressive, liberal, erudite, persuasive rhetoric and lags far behind its words. Apart from singular leadership and weak activist religious groups, established religion and its leadership postures social distancing. The primary reason for this response is "being pastoral" to both sides of the issue. Both the religious and secular establishments routinely ignore thorough scientific, social analysis settling on weak solutions that are palliative and ameliorative for preserving "law and order." This institutional approach robs the people's breath, weakens the will, and extinguishes hope in the heart of the people's movement for change. The religious establishment's fallback rationale is the humdrum cliché of separation of politics and religion. In a liberal capitalist democracy, in as much things change, they remain the same. According to the New York Times, the wealthiest 1% still possess more power than the bottom 90%. In terms of poor people benefits from institutional capitalism, the Pareto Principle of 20% over 80% applies. Blacks in the USA account for 12% of the population. Still, Blacks occupy only 3.2% of the senior positions at large companies in the US.

The question remains. Why does the majority still bear the brunt of the pain and suffering globally, even after the stellar effort of sanctified, charismatic heroes? At different times, Gandhi, Martin Luther King Jr, and Mandela have waged particular heroic actions against corrupt systems that have denied people the breath of life for centuries. Gandhi fought for the release of the British colonial stranglehold on the necks of the Indian people. Martin Luther King Jr led protests against the American racist Republic that applied the knee on its Black people, denying them the right to breathe freely. Mandela violently and non-violently fought for freedom from the yoke of the English/Afrikaner racist Republic of South Africa for the majority voiceless Blacks. Using Gandhi's philosophy of Satyagraha, passive, non-violent passive resistance, they courageously and successfully managed to raise a groundswell of organic protest.

History clearly shows that violence produces substantial progress. Every successful revolution is a case in point. Passive non-resistance around the negotiation communion table delivers reform, cheap peace, and very little justice. The powerful at the table always manage to preserve their interests. Hindsight provides a 20/20 vision of how things work. The question remains: Why do millions across the world still tramp the streets, dancing to the beat of rubber bullets, flash-balls, and tear-gas, singing songs of freedom? And bureaucracy systematically successfully pushes back to the status quo of the glorious days of violent slavery, chattel labor, capitalism, colonialism, classism, casteism, and patriotic nationalism. Let the truth be told.

The uncovering of history proves that Gandhi consistently led the struggle only on behalf of his paying customers, the wealthy upper caste in India and South Africa. Gandhi remained blind to the suffering of the vast majority of Dalit in India, who he regarded as sub-humans, and "kaffirs" in South Africa. Gandhi stood firm on fundamental bigotrous religious scriptural beliefs that doomed the Dalit and outcast to a life of the "sacred duty." This duty included "caring and cleansing the Brahmin's physical body, repairing their toilets, and removing their shit." This Divine mandated scriptural custom continues today. When Gandhi spoke of India for all, he only meant the rich and not dark Dalits and poor outcasts.

Blacks in South Africa, according to Gandhi's religion, belonged to the caste of the outcast. He used the derogatory term "kaffir," used by the British and Afrikaner for Blacks. Gandhi chose to associate with the rich Indians in South Africa, a behavior he carried to India.

Martin Luther King Jr. analyzed the social condition correctly in the USA, making the connection between Capitalism, Imperialism, Racism, and the violence of the Vietnam War. After his death, even his memory became a social threat. Arundhati Roy noted that Corporations and Foundations watered down King's legacy, message, and social analysis to make it market-friendly and acceptable to the powerful capitalist corporations and foundations. The Corporations and foundations promote King's name loudly, carefully emphasizing his passive resistance strategy for the sake of cheap peace. King was adamantly against violence, but these Corporations ironically cooperate and work closely with the Department of Defense, the Armed Forces Chaplains Board, and other violent agencies. Today, corporate-sponsored liberal lectures under King's legacy promote capitalism as a good strategy for promoting non-violent social change. Corporations globally encourage violence and death for profit. King stood for significant change in a violent world; still, the status quo catalyzes the present marches.

Nelson Mandela was canonized as a saint in South Africa after he deferred to the Washington consensus by disappearing Socialism from the ANC's agenda. South Africa's peaceful transitional negotiation ignored the cries of the impoverished resulting in no land reforms, no demands for reparation, no nationalization of the assets such as the lucrative South African mines, power plants, etc. The country's holdings either remain controlled by private entities or bought by individuals or private corporations. Mandela bestowed the prestigious Order of Good Hope on his old friend and supporter General Suharto, the killer of millions of Communists in Indonesia. Before his death, Chris Hani, the ANC youth leader killed by a White assassin, noticed that Mercedes driving former radicals and trade unionists now rule the country. The following poem concisely captures the foolhardy, pious, self-righteous non-violent struggle that preserves capitalism, waged by disingenuous, ignorant leadership on behalf of the suffering voiceless victims. The Nobel peace laureate Archbishop Desmond Tutu, championing the cause of solidarity with the poor and social welfare, flew in Coca-Cola's corporate jet when in the USA. For liberal leaders, the adage *half a loaf is better than none* applies.

SATYAGHRA FOR CAPITALISM

Gandhi practiced semen retention
Did Mandela practice masturbation?
Both benefited from systemic filthy lucre capitalization
Pimping the least of the population.
And Tutu?
Righteous, holy, contemplative, pastoral action?
Riding on a Coca-Cola Jet

Many respected and admired Gandhi's philosophy of *Satyagraha,* the philosophy of non-violent passive resistance. Gandhi also taught the philosophy of *Hind Swaraj,* the self-disciplining house rule that promises personal and social self-rule. Hind Swaraj was the strategy for India's liberation from the British for only the wealthy and upper caste. *Hind Swaraj* included the practice of celibacy and learning the technique of semen retention. As the saying goes, Gandhi mastered this technique with his grandniece lying next to him.

Many Hindus and some Christians proclaimed Gandhi as the historical Christ of the day. Gandhi as the Christ cannot compare with Jesus the Christ. Jesus, unlike Gandhi, had no Imperial Capital backing for his divine mandated mission against the Mammon of capitalism and its Imperial institutions. Jesus had no support from wealthy, bureaucratic institutions. Gandhi, unlike Jesus, hated and struggled against justice and peace for the poor, namely, the Black Dalits, outcast tribes in India, Africans, and low-caste Indians in South Africa. Jesus championed the cause of all who were powerless in the Roman Empire, including Palestinians.

Disregarding the ideological portrayal of tradition's conceptual Jesus, no one liked the historical Jesus of Nazareth. And there never will be. Jesus of Nazareth was born, lived, and died. The rest is 2000 years of theological imagination. The uniqueness of Jesus of Nazareth was that he was an incarnation of the spirit of God, the universal Christ. This Christ is also resident in the spirit body of all humans, regardless of tribal religion and cultural differences. Christ has no favorites but favors the poor. The Christ in Jesus led an organic grassroots struggle against Imperial capitalism, the mother of all social evils. The Romans in Jesus' day pursued a global colonial project of subjugation and exploitation of the world.

This imperial capitalist Colonial Project continues in this present era. It turns God's children into a ghost commodity of exploited chattel "gravediggers" for profit, providing essential services in a divided society. The project also messes up God's world by destroying dams, rivers and exploiting Mother Earth for its valuable possessions. Like in the case of Martin Luther King Jr, Jesus's message of non-violence and repudiation of Imperial Capitalism is muted by sacred and secular bureaucratic institutions. Corporate-sponsored Sunday sermons under Jesus's legacy hypocritically promote the Colonialist Project as an age for non-violent social change. James Baldwin complained that institutional Christianity disarmed the struggle for Black freedom in America. No wonder intelligent youth flee the sacred buildings and do real church by marching in public -in marketplaces and streets on Sundays.

Jesus of Nazareth discerned that Ego lies at the root of the dysfunctional human condition. The Ego is the creator of the Colonial Project globally and is the primary cause of pandemic suffering. The Ego's chief strategy is division and privation. The global Capitalist Project produces slavery and racism in the world.

Jesus identified the Ego/ Self as the Deceiver, the Divider, and the Denier of equity and equitable justice for all. The success of Jesus's message and strategy for the world's welfare hinges primarily on the loss of Ego, solidarity, and reliance on God's grace for the transformation into a new kind of being, full of love and compassion. Jesus passionately championed the cause of the poor, preferred alternative Spartan life, lived off the grid and at the edge of egoist civilization. He was skeptical of the institutional, hierarchical, pyramid scheme of structural controlling power. Jesus modeled a successful movement that was a social, decentralized, inclusive, organic, collective community. He preached the Kingdom of God, only known to the mystic. The kingdom was not anything like any known earthly kingdom. It is a domain of liminal space for prayer, reflective learning, prescient knowledge, wisdom, walking with God, and living with grace for loving action for the welfare of self and others.

In this day and age, the dissemination of previously hidden knowledge catalyzes organic grassroots movements to change the corrupt egoist systems and structures. The internet and Web, new literature, and social connections and conversations energize and motivate the younger generations for the greater good for change in the corrupt world. Jesus encouraged discipleship understood as learning. Jesus modeled a revolutionary strategy for personal and social change. He taught the way of dying to the self/ Ego for transformation. He said: *Unless a grain of wheat falls into the ground and dies, it cannot bear fruit.* His philosophy embodied unconditional love inclusive of extreme sacrifice and material loss. Jesus was uncomfortable with hierarchical power, gush-up economics, and plutocracy. He called his followers friends who would die for the survival of others.

No leadership present and past come close to what Jesus modeled. The world still waits for a Messiah, unlike the illusions we have thus far seen.

FOUR

. . . .

Exceptionalism is one of the primary reasons for social unrest in a dysfunctional society. This divisive egoist standard modus operandi is the chief humanist strategy for power grasp and management through dysfunctional social institutions in the sacred and secular sphere. Yet, all religions encounter a universal spirit familiar to all and known by several names. In the Christian tradition, the energy is the Christ, known as the "anointed one," the Messiah in Jewish tradition. The universal Christ, the essential nature of God, is unconditional love, a natural mutual experience that transcends the exceptionalist mindset.

Christ, the only Way of Love?

The Collect Prayer[1]

*Grant us entirely to know thy Son Jesus Christ to be
the way, the truth, and the life that we may steadfastly
follow his steps that lead to eternal life.*

In this Collect, Jesus is the perfect model for all Christians. But which Jesus? Only God, the universal Christ, is the way, truth, and life for *all*. The Collect does not tell how the son Jesus of Nazareth became Christ, and *the* model of God's way, truth, and life.

Traditional explanations will not lead us to know who Jesus was. Historians of the day are of very little help. Church traditions have deliberately painted their unique tribal cultural picture. Only the disciplined journey back into the Synoptic gospels, namely Mark. Matthew and Luke will bring us close to knowing the man Jesus and his perfect way of the truth and life. Journeying into the earlier gospels will help uncover the many layers of tradition and yield answers to some of the crucial questions surrounding the man Jesus, his message, and his work. This task is necessary and critical for truth, human spiritual growth, transformation, and loving action to heal the broken world effectively.

Many use a literalist approach to the sacred text and deliberately manipulate the words to suit natural egoist inclinations and thoughts that usually translate into meanness towards others. The fact is that we become what we believe about God and Jesus. Jesus rarely behaved meanly, if at all. His way was love. He avoided hurting others unnecessarily. The lifestyle of Jesus generally embraced the way of Gandhi- the idea of *Satyagraha*, the path of non-violence towards others for justice before peace. Paradoxically, *Satyagraha* usually ends in violence to the victim, avoiding all costs of hurt to others. Jesus followed *Satyagraha,* laying down his life by dying a violent death. Those in power avoid *Satyagraha* as a rule.

The violence of the Cross reveals God as unconditional love in a violent world where people live by the sword. God's spirit, the universal Christ, took on bodily form in the man Jesus of Nazareth, revealing the common way God works in history. Paul saw God's spirit in operation in the congregation of Galatia as the fruits, pieces of God's essential nature, given for solidarity and healthy relationships. These fruits include charity, joy, peace, patience, kindness, goodness, faithfulness, gentleness, and self-control- describing the essence and meaning of love. The one who possesses God's essential nature of the fruits does not need the law. For Paul, that person has God, the universal spirit, within and beyond tribal, cultural religion.

We live in a divided world. Egoist religion, and its dogmatic beliefs, have contributed faithfully and facilitated Ego's global plan of divisive conflict and violence in the human condition. Someone correctly once said: *Everything was all right until religion came along.* Jesus never intended that his campaign of universal love should become a premier institution of religion. He had learned personally from his bitter and painful experiences in the local synagogue in his village. On one visit to the local synagogue, strictly religious people forced him to run the gauntlet, intent on killing him by throwing him off the cliff. The religious folk did not hate Jesus because he disrespected their beliefs, rituals, laws, and sacrifices. Nor did they hate Jesus because he claimed to be God, as some said. Religious folk hated Jesus precisely for pointing out the Decalogue's foundational principle of unconditional love. Jesus summarized the Book of Leviticus based on the two tablets of the Law as unconditional love for God and neighbor. The Ten Commandments, the two tablets of the Law, mean unconditional love for all. *And all means all.* Tennessee Williams said: *If you want to piss people off, you can do two things: Attain some happiness or tell the truth.* Jesus attained the highest yogic state of bliss and spoke the truth from the depths of God. This bliss pissed off that little incorporated village community drowning in transactional love mediated through legalist religion.

Love is a mystery, especially the love that is the essence of God. In the Greek language, God's love, the agape' kind, is the only real thing in this world. "Real" means that which is not temporary, not corrupt, but eternal. God's love is God, for only God is eternal. Everything else is illusory and has a brief shelf life. "Corrupt" in its original sense means "not everlasting." Everything created by Ego is corrupt, including civilization, its cultural religion, etc. The crown of Ego's creations, the Empire, lasts for approximately 500 years.

The Collect brings three words together- Son, Jesus, Christ. Church tradition reads the traditional doctrine of incarnation into the early

Greek sacred scriptures. In the Synoptic gospels of Mark, Matthew, and Luke, the initial understanding of Jesus as Son, Savior, Messiah, King, and Christ differs from tradition's conceptual beliefs about Jesus the man, his message, and work. The institutional Church believes in the God-man, equating the man Jesus with God, or above God. This belief has removed God from the salvation of humankind, and God's participation in removing the only Sin, the sin of apostasy, in the human condition. The atonement theory blames human shortcomings on the scapegoat Jesus excusing the sinner of personal responsibility for the sins he has committed. In the earlier gospels, Jesus's message focuses on the cause of social unrest and dysfunction rather than the symptoms. Jesus's kerygma taught the spirituality of loss of the self/ Ego that has captured the human mind and subdued ab-original conscience. Jesus also taught his disciples the way of contemplative prayer- living in God in a Liminal Space where grace is freely available for the God kind of life in this world. Jesus did not teach anything original. This spiritual path is the way taught by mystics in all religious traditions globally. This way of Jesus was perceived by the "religious" as a threat, foreign, and subversive.

Baptism originally was the plan for helping people traumatized by the apocalyptic events of the times. People's personal lives were falling apart. John and Jesus offered a baptism for crossing over from the old to the new, making room inside the mind and soul for love, solidarity, vision, purpose, expansion, and hope. The church baptizes neophytes for participation in *God Wars*. Believers, armed with the doctrinal Jesus in one hand, and the Biblical sword in the other, energized by Ego's disingenuous transactional love, sow seeds of division and deprivation of God's grace and communion. Toxic tribal religion spreads like herpes upon the earth, sowing global pain, suffering, and death. Institutional religion, aligned with the State, actively and passively, conspire to birth spawn for division, exploitation, and destruction of the planet.

Some progressive evangelicals in the USA have criticized other extremist fundamentalist evangelicals for their sociopathic tendencies since 1970. The way of Jesus, the practice of unconditional love, never sanctioned fear, hatred, prejudice, inhospitality, and violence against those outside the tribal God's religion or those seeking asylum from other countries.

The Collect, at a glance, suggests that Christ is the last name of Jesus, the man from Nazareth. Many in Christendom believe strongly that this is true. Christ cannot the last name of the man from Nazareth. Christ refers to God, who is spirit, which existed before the creation of time and space. The man from Nazareth was born sometime between 6 and 4 years before the common era. Jesus's divinity happened as an evolving thought by councils and decided by the Church between 325 CE and 451 CE. In his book, How Jesus became God, Bart D. Ehrman sketches Jesus's transformation from a human prophet to the son of God and exalted to divine status at his resurrection. He concludes that Jesus of Nazareth was not born God. The institution, convinced by few early followers who could write, made Jesus God. In the earlier scriptures, Christ and Jesus are inextricably connected merely as a loving father and obedient son, but not uniquely related by essence. "Christ" refers directly to God as creator alone and is God's fulfilled word in John's gospel. Paul always equates Christ with God in his letters, and like all Jews, would not entertain another God equal to God, sitting beside God. Luke, the bibliographer of Paul, comparing Paul and Jesus, men working and suffering for God, notes that Paul superseded Jesus.

The Cosmos, saturated with the universal spirit, needs no personified intermediary, religious institutions, cleric, or belief to access God's love. Humans possess the indwelling presence of God since the creation event billions of years ago. We do ourselves a great disservice to separate "Christ" from God. The cup of water from the ocean is the same water in the sea. We do ourselves short when we believe that God or Christ can live only in the Christian camps' traditional beliefs about the man

Jesus from Nazareth. God and Christ are the same, but Jesus is another story, just one historical incarnation of many.

God did not incarnate in the world only once in the historical birth of Jesus of Nazareth. God incarnated on this earth as far back as 4.5 billion years ago. And before that, God extended God's essence as love in the Cosmos, the grand initial creation event at the Big Bang 13,8 billion years ago. God incarnated in Primates between 2 million and 1.8 million years ago. No one knows when the Day of Pentecost happened then. According to the mystic John, God in Christ embodies every child coming into this world in real-time. Everyone, not just Jesus of Nazareth, is uniquely Christ. Everything organic and inorganic pulsates with Christ, God's breath, and God's life-giving spirit of sustenance, renewal, and unconditional love.

All humans, by God's act of creation, are the embodiment of Christ. All children, by natural birth, are enlightened and possess Christ. These truths help us assume a humble posture when speaking to those especially about sectarian tribal beliefs. Unlike many past and present missionaries, Jesus modeled a compassionate approach in his healing ministry. Jesus did not take God to others. He was joyfully surprised to find God already present in those he visited. Paul, preaching in the Areopagus, discovered God was already with the Athenians. Jesus did not have a master/ servant/ pagan relationship with others. He called them his friends. Jesus sat down with people, drank with them, and associated with prostitutes. When he looked into the eyes of people, he saw the face of God. He was not patronizing when he taught them how-to live-in union with God. Jesus learned first from others before teaching. St. Francis also advised: *Seek first to understand before being understood.*

God and Christ are the same. And God is unconditional love. In a pluralist world, the Collect must emphasize mirroring unconditional love and solidarity with others.

The perfect way modeled by the man Jesus was the lifestyle of God's love for all the Beloved. For too long, this wonderful Collect based on the sacred scriptures has been misunderstood, abused, manipulated, and claimed by one esoteric eschatological cultural group. Many well-meaning zealous evangelists disingenuously massage the text of the Collect to mean: *My Jesus is the only way, the only truth, the only life.* In the marketplace of religion, these beliefs function as an accelerant in the global theater of the *God Wars.* Without God's love, the egoist mind raises heroes, shapes ideas into weapons of mass destruction of others, and bombs ancient civilizations into the ground. Unconditional love will always win because unconditional love, the only eternal reality in a disappearing world, cannot die. This love will always bear a rich harvest of good. No human heart in any cultural religion or civilization can withstand the universal God and Christ's influence of unconditional love. God's unconditional love is the only eternal reality on this planet and remains the truth referred to in the Collect. In the hymn of love, St. Paul sings the triumph of love. He states three things that abide forever in this world- faith, hope, and love, but the greatest is love. Jesus showed us the perfect way to union with this truth, the God of love who brings blissful joy, fulfillment, justice, and peace to others.

Jiddhu Krishnamurthi advises against egoist religion that proposes transactional love.

> *Put away the book, the description, the tradition, the authority,*
> *and take the journey of self-discovery. Love, and don't be caught in*
> *opinions and ideas about what love is or should be. When you love,*
> *everything will come right. Love has its action. Love, and you will*
> *know the blessings of it. Keep away from the authority who tells*

you what love is and what it is not. No establishment knows, and
he who knows he cannot tell. Love, and there is understanding.

In his letter, John, the apostle of love, encourages the kind of love that translates into the truth of laying down one's life for others, the love that is real action beyond words. Society typically organizes on the Hegelian dialectic of master-slave for control and domination. The practice of Jesus's radical love depends on the death of Ego. Also, one must die daily to self and take up the new way of living in God. This life miraculously happens when one kneels before the altar dedicated to gods made by humans, encounters God, sacrifices selfish interests, and practices mindful compassion for others and the planet.

FIVE

Most countries embrace capitalism, the mother of all social dysfunction, disease, and death in the corrupt human condition. Humans and the planet are always the casualties in the capitalist Colonial Project based on greed for profit. Capitalism, a virulent disease, infects both the sacred and secular world. So, what can save humans from hysteria, the natural product of social unrest and dis-ease?

Keeping Alert

And that, knowing the time, that now it is high time to awake out of sleep: for now, is our salvation nearer than when we first believed.

The dictionary definition of colonization is *the action or process of settling among and establishing control over an area's indigenous people.* Historical empires in several eras have colonized vast tracts of land for capitalist interest. Empires and kingdoms are flawed because they are human created, therefore corrupt, unreal, consequently temporary. They have a limited shelf life of plus or minus 500 years.

The present Empire, the USA, aligns with multinational corporations for global economic control of the world. In this worldwide neo-colonialist project, local governments are allowed to manage their affairs according to the demands of these massive corporations.

Under Mandela's leadership, the African National Congress (ANC), before assuming control of South Africa's government, had to defer to Washington DC, the epicenter of the global economy. The ANC promised to replace capitalism in the struggle for freedom with a social program to relieve South Africa's majority. Mandela and his team at the negotiation were surprised by a hostage situation. The deal did not include the social agenda. Their leaders peacefully negotiated away demands of land reforms, reparations, and general welfare. The corporations allowed Mandela to structure a new government that would relate to the corporations as a nation-state. This structure made it possible for white owners partnered with global corporations to control the country's economy. The status quo of wealth distribution, the Pareto Principle, still applies in South Africa- 20% super-rich whites and 80% middle-class and poor. The present situation is slightly changing as new leadership break ceilings and empty the treasury. Former radical poor freedom fighters are now driving Mercedes Benzes, and trade unionists now govern South Africa. South Africa ranks as the 9th worst country globally for unemployment. South Africa typifies what happens globally with nation-states controlled by liberal corporate capitalism.

Capitalism smartly works through multinational corporations, Foundations (Rockefeller, Carnegie, Ford), banks (World Bank, International Monetary Fund), and National Government Agencies (NGOs) at the local outposts through welfare projects. Corporations strongly influence national governments, even the UNO, and have been known to use threats of defunding. NGOs on the ground encourage blind allegiance and acceptance of the ideology and programs of their funders. The multi-national corporations divide and rule by caste, class, and race. In the Center for Talent Innovation's *Being Black in Corporate America*" report in 2018, Blacks accounted for only 3.2% of large corporations' senior roles. Blacks hold 0.8% of Fortune 500 Chief Executor Officer positions.

International Foundations use NGOs to preserve the status quo for the sake of cheap peace. NGOs focus on turning potential protestors into paid loyal activists. They pacify talented artists, intellectuals, and moviemakers, especially those who agree not to be aggressive and silent about injustices. They play a crucial part in financing a conceptual coup that transforms the idea of justice into human rights. This narrow focus blocks paying attention to the larger picture, the social, political, and economic context. Gender, pandemic poverty, and racism, shorn of its social, political, and economic context, become identity crises. Women, the poor, and those who are Black, and Brown do not have an identity crisis. These human problems exist because of the lack of power and directly connect to capitalism, the root cause, the mother of social dysfunction.

Foundations in the USA fling money at intelligent, technologically gifted people who cleverly transform people's suffering into corporate profit. In India, the film industry profited from poverty in the movie *Slum Dog Millionaire*. Corporations co-opt Martin Luther King Jr's name and strategy of passive resistance in the USA, packaging a message to disarm and disempower a violent liberation struggle. In the USA and South Africa, Black Consciousness marches on by using Black consciousness to sell *blackness* with consumer goods.

Capitalism destroys the planet. The old policies that have dug themselves out of past crises, namely war, and shopping, do not seem to be working. Trickle-down economics has failed the poor. The profit pathway is always upwards into the political elite's pocket— and the wealthiest 1% own 99% of the world's wealth.

Interrogating Systemic Racism and the White Academic Field uncovered that higher learning institutions experience the same capitalist, racist dynamics within the Academy. Corporations working through institutional bureaucracy defund or poorly fund department offerings in fields of study in Africana Studies, Asian American and Pacific Islander Studies, Native American Studies, Latinx Studies, and related areas. There exists systemic racism, and anti-Blackness within these institutions of learning demonstrated in department funding and staffing. The gap between the antiracist project of ethnic studies and the liberal arts and sciences project remains remarkable. Many are ignorant of the White Academic Front (WAF) and White Academic Power (WAP) in higher learning institutions. Dependence on liberal philanthropy robs dignity, preserves the status quo policies, and keeps the discriminatory structures. The institution is held hostage to a conceptual coup. Fortunately, in South Africa, easy access to information alerts informs and serves as an organic driving force for change. Recently, books, buildings, and sacred effigies have gone up in flames during protest demonstrations.

In the United States and Africa, new Black Evangelicals using a suspicious hermeneutic complain that the Colonial Project used religion to whiten their skins. This Project has succeeded in subduing or erasing African culture, including primal traditional religion, stealing the Black mind. These emerging Evangelicals know that God was in Africa long before the colonial missionaries brought foreign tribal religion and culture to thriving African Empires. Black intellectual evangelical ministers' research raises questions about Jesus's existence and the gospels' fabrication. White emergent ministers within mainline evangelicalism such as Brian D. McLaren, Tony Jones, Doug Paget, Kester Brewin, and Peter Rollins question the fundamentals of Evangelical tradition. They also disbelieve traditional doctrines that place Jesus, the man, central to the work of God's salvation, and above God, and God's mission in the world today. Western Protestant thinkers like Phyllis Tickle, Diana Butler Bass, Don Cuppit, and theologian Bart Ehrman question 2000 years of traditional church history. These scholars make a solid case, concluding that the institutional church turned Jesus the man into

God and deviated from the man Jesus's central message, especially in the early gospels.

The mystics, who left the traditional church in the 3rd and 4th Centuries, could not tolerate the church becoming an institution of religion. They accused the church of reducing God to a concept that practices social distancing. In learning institutions in the West, White Academic Power exists. In White's institutional church, Theological Power continues the Colonial Project's capitalist mission and the Balkanization of the Black ethnic mind, body, heart, and God. The State keeps the people hungry, and the church holds the people humble. North Atlantic Western Theology dominates Liberation Theology and disfavors those on the underside of Capitalist history. The idea of separation of Church and State, or alignment with the State, brings no timely relief to the powerless poor in capitalist society.

The bureaucracy of the institutional Church will continue to solve its egoist, disingenuous plans for systemic division and deprivation, especially power. The church's progressive rhetoric has always fallen far ahead of its feet. The liberal generosity evident in its justice programs and projects preserve the status quo. Round table conferences, seminars, and discussion groups will purposely ignore the broader social, political, and economic context. Systemic racism, poverty, and gender will degrade into an identity problem. Pious prayers expressing vain hope will rise like incense to express false hope that "good governance" will resolve grievances.

Society generally is unaware of the effects of capitalist colonization, its captivity of people's minds, and its propensity and massive power to create and sustain global servitude, poverty, disease, and widespread destruction of the planet. Capitalist and Religious corporations use propaganda and theology, invest tons of money into smartness to operate fearful strategies to control and suppress the Truth. The result- preserving the status quo, safeguarding official policies and doctrines for reformation rather than deformation. Christendom ignores the teaching of its founder Jesus who radically preached deformation, death, and dying for the new way of living in God's kingdom.

Karl Marx stated that religion is the opiate to the people. He said this in capitalist industrial society, where the super-wealthy exploited the abject poor in France. In the context of Imperial colonial capitalism, Paul encouraged the church to keep alert or awake. Some say Karl Marx was wrong, but we cannot disbelieve the traditional orthodox truth of the saint of the institutional Church. Paul said in the letter to the Romans:

> *And that, knowing the time, that now it is*
> *high time to awake out of sleep: for now, is our*
> *salvation nearer than when we first believed.*

From the underbelly of history, the ghosts of the dead rise, lamenting nothing much has changed. Paul advises: *Do not conform to this world's pattern but transform by renewing your mind. Then you will be able to test and approve what God's good, pleasing, and perfect will is.*

First things first, there is much unlearning and learning to do. Let us know that the time is now, and it is high time to wake out of sleep as learners/ disciples of Christ.

SIX

....

*The arrogant Empire in the West assumes a God-ordained
mission to be a beacon of light to the world. Under the authority
of this mandated call, the Empire commissions and sends its
ideologues of Democracy and Liberal Capitalists into the world.
The corporate owners of global Capitalism are a secret cabal of
wheelers and dealers. They do their dirty work at international,
national states, or international outposts. In long dark corridors, the
conspiracy secretly and privately cut deals to satiate egoic corporate
desires and needs for wealth and power. In partnership with
Corporations, the Empire aims to accumulate corporate capital,
no matter the human cost or the planet's destruction. How did Jesus
respond to the Empire and its unquenchable hunger and thirst for
filthy lucre? Can we learn anything from the narratives of the teacher
Jesus in the Western scriptures? What type of religion, if any, suits the
Capitalist world. This sermon explains the phenomenon of Capitalism,
its beginnings. It also identifies its various forms, its operation, and effects
in the modern world. Finally, this essay proposes a spirituality that works
as an effective vaccine against the virus of contemporary capitalism.*

The God of Mammon

On his visit to the Temple before his crucifixion, Jesus
noticed that some had set up tables to sell small animals
for sacrificial rites and Temple money to purchase these
offerings. The idea that some would profit from religion and others,

especially the poor, disturbed him deeply. He was visibly shaken and appeared disgusted and angry. Some white commentators who usually have trouble with black anger in the world manage to kindly judge this Black man's response as "righteous anger." The Evangelists usually present Jesus as meek and mild. Some commentators have no problem with Jesus behaving like a human, state that Jesus acted violently in this story. He made a whip of cords and drove out the scoundrels who had made the house of God a marketplace, a den of thieves bent on profiteering off the powerless poor.

In his famous Sermon on the Mount, he preached that one could not serve the world's two masters- God and Mammon. Mammon, a Syrian deity, is a Biblical metaphor denoting the human propensity to pursue wealth rather than serve the bigger self, God, or neighbor. The Bible warns that *the love of money is the root of all kinds of evil, for which some have strayed from the faith in their greediness and pierced themselves through with many sorrows.*

Traditional Christianity condemns the *love* of money as a sin. Many, tempted by the lure and the greedy pursuit of money, live with uncontrollable compulsions- paranoid hysterics and perversions- unconscious of the soul's deepest longing for union with God, compassionate love for neighbor, and humanity. The love of money leads to the existential loss of personal integrity, loss of spiritual cooperation and solidarity with God, others, other creatures, and the world. The egoist misdirected false self mentally creates and unleashes egoic systems and structures upon the earth. These religious, political, and economic structures of governance foster and sustain a dysfunctional society where social hysteria, hunger, poverty, disease, and death run rampant globally.

The many Biblical narrative texts and established religion have still not deterred believers from the idolatrous practice of the love of money.

Corporate Christian evangelists go out into the world to sell capitalism in all its malleable forms. Capitalism is the proverbial wolf in sheep's clothing and has the plastic ability to morph into many hybrid forms. Capitalism considers greed and avarice as necessary evils for the sake of civilization's progress. The majority suffer or die for the entitled few. The ethic of love, the humanity of the soul, the moral life, and the preservation of the planet are expedient oblations on the God of Mammon's altar for profit. Now a pandemic virus, capitalism unleashes division, illness, death, destruction, and deprivation in the world. The sacrificial knife of Capitalism slices and dices humankind into caste, class, and race in the global mess, competing for social contradictions and cultural identities. Each year's capitalist harvest of profit hides countless dead losses and a host of ghostly witnesses.

Capitalism has its roots firmly in Christian theology. In his book, <u>The Protestant Ethic and the Spirit of Capitalism,</u> Max Weber's thesis postulates that the Calvinistic individualistic Christian ethic of hard work for progress led to the creation and success of Capitalism's ideology. Christians fail or refuse to ask: *How can a system with such a social tone of Darwinism, cannibalism, and violence be compatible with Christianity's sacrificial love ethic?* Jesus's *satyagraha* did not condone violence, especially of the kind and magnitude of modern liberal capitalism.

What is the state of Capitalism today? Slavoj Zizek, a Slovenian philosopher and international director of the Birkbeck Institute, rightly states that Christianity and Christianity's Confucian ethic of the Golden Rule is incompatible with Capitalism. He suggests changing the title of Weber's book. In Zizek's opinion, the title should be <u>The Darwinian Protestant Ethic and the Spirit of Capitalism</u>. Christian Protestant ethics has nothing to do with the spirit of capitalism. An article in the *Sojourners* penned by Stephen Mattson, dated January 25, 2017, entitled *American Christianity has Failed,* points out convincingly the point made in the title. Western Christianity looks nothing like Jesus nor his philosophy of life. Jesus's gospel instructed his followers to help the poor, oppressed, maligned, mistreated, sick, and those most in need.

American Christianity powerfully influences those stationed at the local, national, and current Empire's colonial capital outposts worldwide. In the USA, American Christianity has rejected refugees, refused aid to immigrants, kidnapped immigrant children, cut social services to those snagged in poverty, withheld help for the sick, fueled xenophobia, reinforced misogyny, ignored racism, stoked hatred, increased corruption, inequality, prejudice, and fear. Many Christians refuse to use their political advocacy and options to apply Jesus's summary of the Law, the Golden Rule of love for neighbor and self. In the Trump era, Christians were more worried about losing money, power, influence, and control than about living the gospel of love, learning, humility, sacrifice, and generosity. Because of Capitalism's Babylonian Captivity of the God of Love, one can expect not much change in future governance in the USA. The narrative of Ego's narcissistic fear and ideology of capitalism in the Empire has successfully negated the Jesus gospel of unconditional love for the love of money and bending the knee in obedience at the altar to the God of Mammon.

The ubiquitous pain and suffering in the modern world stem from the Empire's capitalistic grasp and exploitation of the world. Most are oblivious that everything in the contemporary era connects to liberal capitalism, the present form. People are generally more prone to focus on the individual or local hysterical issues like race, gender, etc., churned up by social unrest. The Western heart and mind believe that Capitalism is the better of all other economic systems, especially evil socialism. Socialism and Communism are the greatest fear of most in the West. Western propaganda touts Socialism and Communism as losing the Christian God, cultural tradition, and ethics.

Capitalism in the world combines power and money. This combination becomes a potent cocktail mix for gross social atrocities, loss of life as idle enjoyment, and gross exploitation of the natural world. In India, Capitalism encourages the rise of nationalism, dominance of language and religious fundamentalism. Orthodox trading and modern farming have significantly changed the social and natural landscape. Colossal Corporate infrastructure projects have displaced hundreds of thousands of rural poor, sending them adrift into the world that refuses to respect, recognize, or care for them. The USA capitalist gratuitous wars and sanctioned greed jeopardize and fill the world cities with refugees who flock to neighboring India from Pakistan and China. In India's seven-year war with Afghanistan, thousands have lost their lives. The whole region has descended into chaos amidst the desolation and rubble of ancient cities pounded into the dust. Global international corporations attack forests, rivers, crops, seeds, farmers, labor laws, and policymaking. The work against climate change is now at the state's convenience and declared a security challenge in India. The State deems as terrorists those who stay to husband the land, defend and resist expulsion, protest treasonable offenders. The government's genius solution will involve buying and selling, more consumerism, and profiteering by fewer people. In other words, more Capitalism. Indian farmers are allowed to purchase seeds only from Corporations at exorbitant, unaffordable prices.

The Elephant in the room in the modern era is capitalism. A single umbilical cord connects all social contradictions and cultural identities to capitalism in this global hysterical mess. Those involved in the struggle for justice do not go deep enough to destroy Capitalism's root. The branches of populist issues survive pruning and come back stronger. Observers say those Liberals who focus on binary and individual cultural identity issues focus on the fig leaves covering the tree of Capitalism. The tree has a root- Liberal Capitalism.

Without conscience, the West has accepted the propaganda that capitalism is a virtuous system, a necessary evil, or the best in comparison. The Christian belief that Christ died so that Capitalism may rise is not too far-fetched in the evangelical USA. The Catholic *Doctrine of Discovery,* which justified the European conquest of the Americas and the African slave trade, offered spiritual validation for European domination and colonial capitalist exploitation. The same Discovery Doctrine of colonialism strongly influences the Modern Evangelical Protestant Church. The Church pursues capitalism with the same passion declaring Caucasian bodies as superior and Black and Brown bodies inferior. The doctrine relegates natives of lands "discovered" as "outsiders," unwelcome, and permitted to exist mainly as chattel and the cheap labor force.

Dead but still relevant in the modern world, Karl Marx defined Capitalism as a "mode of production." This definition of capitalism has evolved in the modern era. It emerged from previous modes to become, by as early as 1848, a global system of unrivaled energy and economic prowess. The bourgeoisie, by the payment system for labor, now enjoy economic and social control over the proletariat, the labor force. Yet, despite many superficial changes, Capitalism remains the same exploitation, oppression, and alienation from power. The labor force, identified as the "gravediggers of capitalism," remains the only revolutionary hope for a just, socialist world. Marx said: *It is not the consciousness of men that determines their being, but on the contrary, their social being determines their consciousness. (Preface to A Contribution to the Critique of Political Economy, 1859.)*

Karl Marx believed in Hegelian dialectics- that labor would negate its opposite Capitalism. A more advanced society, socialism: an organization run by the direct producers for human need would disappear from capitalist class distinctions and, ultimately, class society's abolition. For Marx, hope for a fair, just future and advanced civilization depends solidly on the proletariat's will. The proletariat possesses and controls the grassroots power for change and progress. Marx's description that the working class consists of most of the neediest, most exploited does not exist today. Today's society, therefore, cannot generate a powerful revolution against Capitalism. Society is differently structured than in Marx's day. Only strong national states organized transnationally can bring about significant change in the world. In local situations, competing social contradictions and binary cultural identities must compromise or lose identity for the common class struggle for an abundant, enjoyable life. Marx identifies the enemy and tells the truth of revolution. The global problem needs a radical response for a new world structure supported by new, sound systems. This same truth Jesus spoke to the Empire when he said: *New Wine, for new wineskins!*

How does global Capitalism work in the modern world? Global Multinational Corporations conduct business with the nation-states and their leaders. The new leaders often find themselves in a novel experience of complex negotiations. When Mandela deferred to Washington, DC, for consultation for regime change in South Africa, corporations threatened to leave with their money and investments. In the negotiations for regime change, corporate America objected to doing business with a government on the brink of a more advanced society based on egalitarian, social reforms based on socialist ideals. Washington DC refused to entertain the idea that South Africa, the direct producers, the proletariat, and the "naked worker" abstracted from the land would return as landowners. Mandela and his weak, ignorant leadership betrayed the ANC Charter's basic tenets when faced with formidable multi-national economic giants at the regime change altar.

South Africa's founding fathers proposed the basic socialist principles that safeguarded the people's dignity, connection to the land, worker rights, and enjoyment of life. The American Empire and global corporations in 1989 would have nothing to do with the people's demand for social happiness. The outcome of the negotiations, the Capitalist Corporations, with local leadership's permission at the national outpost, sowed to the wind. The new South Africa now reaps a whirlwind, the harvest of corruption- corrupt administration, misconduct, the disappearance of abstract wealth, wholesale sell-off of constant capital, and the naked worker's abuse. The wheels of capitalism's machines of Corporations, namely Foundations and landed NGOs run smoothly. Their primary purpose is to defuse radical movements and harness them to the market forces.

An insidious umbilical cord connects capitalism and racism. In the nation-states, the present crisis of violence- colonial and post-colonial-lies embedded in the root of racial Capitalism, the modern ordering, and the administration of human life today. For centuries, this Capitalist matrix has relied on much violence and death to function effectively. According to Michel Foucault, the French philosopher, the modern Capitalist order aims to create citizens of all walks of life. It is malleable enough to appeal and operate efficiently within the divisive capitalist system and even provide the illusion of enjoyment in the broader context of suffering. Modern society "suffers from a paradox of racism that it directs against itself." Racist-Capitalism itself is not a paradox. The coding explains why the new ordering and administering of human life has always relied upon much violence and death to function efficiently. The Cameroonian critical theorist Achille Abembe has named this Capitalist violence "necropolitics." He defines "necropolitics" as "not merely a State's "right" to kill and to organize people to be killed, but also to expose them to extreme violence and death and to reduce entire segments of populations to the barest and most precarious existence." All for the sake of preservation to keep the established economic and political hierarchies of the capitalist system.

How does local government function within modern capitalism? The first Peruvian theorist Anibal Quijano termed "coloniality of power" for business conduction at government centers after decolonization. The same violent, racist, and necropolitical dynamics remain at the heart of colonial governance. In more powerful and wealthy societies like the USA, the discourses will be more racial and exclusively deployed. The government system and its constituency will become more criminal as the proletariat rise in protest. The German philosopher Max Horkheimer first diagnosed the inherent criminal dynamics of modern governance in a Capitalist System. Current governments rest on a relationship of mutual dependency. Those who rule protect and exploit their clients at the same time.

The other function of the repressive State is to wage war. American sociologist Charles Tilly termed "war-making and state-making" simultaneously the highest form of organized crime and the purest form of governance. Modern states and governing structures have shared the same DNA as large-scale criminal enterprises or "rackets" from the start. The power comes from extorting money, resources, and loyalty from communities in return for protection from internal and external threats (which, more often than not, *they, the State,* created or exacerbated).

Capitalism is malleable and possesses the unique ability to morph into other hybrid forms according to need and greed. With European Imperialism, American expansionism, and two world wars, the pendulum swung to decolonization, which produced material prosperity in the West. A type of economic governance called "cuddly Capitalism evolved. Technological advances, "free market" orthodoxy, and neo-conservative political and cultural ideologies created "neo-Liberal Capitalism." The Global South experienced such policies from the start as neocolonialism, given the locus of the heart of colonial power. Narrow segments of society reaped the macroeconomic growth from neo-liberal policies. Simultaneously, corruption, inequality, and criminalized poverty grew significantly, exacerbated by intensified structural racism that undid the gains of the previous era.

The beginning of the 21st Century saw a new kind of politics emerging from neoliberalism- necro politics. Dynamics such as neoliberal market orthodoxies, the "war on terror," direct appeal to racial, ethnic, cultural, religious "pure" identities justified this deadly form of politics. In addition, governance required restrictions for more profound institutionalized corruption in the political, economic, and financial systems. Through it, even more, wealth siphoned to the 1% super-rich.

As inequality, poverty, societal pathologies, debt, disease, addiction, and environmental degradation rose, more liberals began to question the system's morality and viability. As support for character grew, a right ideological trend towards overt racial and cultural politics has reared its ugly head among White conservative Evangelicals. This brand of evangelicals is the traditional American capitalism beneficiaries. They support the political protection "rackets" that dominate conservative-led politics within and outside the country. Religion and economics are a toxic mix in the modern era.

How would Jesus respond to modern biopolitics (control of people) and the contemporary brand of necrocapitalism (greed that destroys people)? Jesus was born and lived when the Roman Empire dominated Judea and Israel. These were colonial outposts of the Roman Empire, national states that existed for exploitation, and bases for the Roman Empire's eastern global expansion. Leadership, both religious and secular, became corrupt. Empire-appointed administration, sacred and secular, functioned as sycophantic pawns pledging blind obedience to authority for self-enrichment. They sold national assets and turned their people into abstract profit as the proletariat. Necro politics and necro-Capitalism dominated the biopolitical context and spread like herpes as the Roman Empire expanded by its comfortable eastward stride.

Jesus taught and practiced the way of detachment to counteract the debasing influence of material wealth. He lived in that in-between space, off the grid, centering on the needs of the "true self," the soul, and the cry of all people in the mess of social contradictions and binary cultural hysteria. Jesus made no distinction or valuation between people and their personal or group struggle. He proposed a way of life in the familiar Imperial capitalist context. His way of life did not encourage retreat from the world of suffering caused by colonial capitalism. Jesus was a mystic who taught his disciples the mystic way of being and becoming a new human. This approach involved kenosis, the loss of Ego's compulsions, the healing of unconsciousness, the ignorance of the self and world. Compulsions explained by Jesus would include the love of money and the destruction and exploitation of others, humans, creatures, and the natural world for profit and wealth. Ego's compulsions create perversion and depression.

The way of Jesus resonates with the timeless primal global tradition of the mystics' yogic ascetic path of training or discipline (*sadhana*) to attain union with God (*samadhi*). Through deep contemplation or meditation, one could live like Jesus in the sacred liminal space of the Advent of God, which Jesus called the Kingdom of God. Jesus retreated continually to this place for graceful strength and wisdom for the practice of love and life in the Ego's world, in solidarity with others, other creatures, and the natural world.

Jesus, like Paul, used social principles for building community. They knew the importance of the practice of solidarity and love for others for social well-being and community (*ubuntu*). They worked and deposited their earnings in a treasury, distributing according to individual needs. Marx copied the phrase "*distribution according to each one's needs*" from Paul. In Matthew 25, socialism was an essential practice of the faith community.

> *[35] For I was hungry, and you gave me food, I was thirsty,*
> *and you gave me drink, was a stranger, and you welcomed*
> *me, [36] I was naked, and you clothed me, I was sick, and*
> *you visited me, I was in prison, and you came to me.'*

Matthew records that the obedient who practice this socialist life will enjoy life in God's kingdom. But, on the other hand, the disobedient will suffer a life of banishment and recurring hellish punishment.

We live in times of disorder, a world was religious, conservative, political Christian's frown upon showing social hospitality. Christian fundamentalist evangelicals, the current beneficiaries of modern necrocapitalism, use rhetoric that labels generous and kind actions as socialist, liberal, evil, and unpatriotic. The USA quickly forgets what remains of Capitalist Conservative Christian Democracy because it is socialist in many respects. Harry S. Truman, 33rd President of the USA, in a speech delivered on October 10, 1952, reminds us of socialism in the USA:

> *Socialism is a scare word they have hurled at every advance the*
> *people have made in the last 20 years. Socialism is what they*
> *call public power. Socialism is what they call social security.*
> *Socialism is what they call farm price supports. Socialism is what*
> *they call bank deposit insurance. Socialism is what they call the*
> *growth of free and independent labor organizations. Socialism*
> *is their name for almost anything that helps all the people.*

Capitalism and Religion cannot be separated. It enjoys the privilege of complete orthodoxy in the Western world. Christianity, integrated into the fabric of imperial politics and governance, holds institutional stock in the political and economic systems. We live in an advanced industrialist capitalist society. In his book, Herbert Marcuse, philosopher, and sociologist, in One_Dimensional Man, analyzed that "the progress of technological rationality is liquidating the oppositional and transcending elements of being human, ethical, and moral "higher culture" in a capitalist society." The Protestant Calvinistic ethic of hard work encouraged a particular brand of individualized spirituality. This era saw the rise of several self-help gurus who taught "how-to" programs.

What type of religious spirituality fits the global culture dominated by Max Weber's Calvinist Protestant Darwinist hard work ethic? Slavoj Zizek, the Slovenian philosopher, recommends a malleable form of spirituality. The nature of capitalism is fragile, subject to depression, pandemic viruses, and continual market crashes. The weaknesses in capitalism render the individual weak and vulnerable to the volatile moods of the market and the whims of a select few. The modern world demands separation from the world's core desire for capitalism. Humankind must strive to be part of something much more extensive and elastic to handle the planet. Zizek diagnoses that the individual in the modern world suffers from a lack of internalized care. He proposes spiritual healing that comes through reflection on the self and broader issues. He judges the self as illusory and that the self is God's image on the individual level. For Zizek, the answer to the human dilemma lies outside of where materialist institutional religion is. Zizek and Steven Weinberg express their skepticism concisely:

> *With or without religion, good people can*
> *behave well, and bad people can do evil; but for*
> *good people to do evil, that takes religion.*

It is only those who practice their beliefs that prove the truth of their ideas. This truthful scientific observation that meaning and purpose emerge from actual life experience contradicts the Western illusion that ideology dictates life. Neils Bohr, the scientist, hung a horseshoe over his entrance door, not because the horseshoe prevented evil from entering his home. He did it because his friend told him that it works. In the

West, ideology is not actual. It is people who practice the illusionary idea that proves the actuality of the concept. Nietzsche stated that there are no Christians. He conceded that there was one Christian, and he died on the cross. Jesus was the only one because he practiced his beliefs. There never were or will be Christians for Nietzsche because they do not practice their ideology.

What religion is profitable and a cure for capitalism? Zizek mentions Buddhism as the type of spirituality that would be helpful in an advanced industrial society. He prefers not the orthodox Buddhism but the popular version making its influence in the West. This type practices self-negation, practical nothingness, and molding self into the world around one. The move in the West is from self-help spirituality to self care, knowledge, and integration (solidarity) with others, other creatures, and the world. In the West, people are moving away from the Christian tradition controlled by the Roman Imperial narrative, the Great Reformation belief in the Bible's authority, the Max Weber Protestant hard-work ethic, and the modern Capitalist movement , towards Taoist inward spirituality.

Zizek is not original by proposing inner spirituality in apocalyptic times. All mystical spirituality has their origins in a world falling apart. There is a suppressed mystical approach within all religions. In the early Christian tradition, Jesus, John the Evangelist, Paul, and other classical and contemporary mystics pointed the same higher path to a nobler culture in the context of the corrupt world. In this tradition, the iconic teachers taught leaving the world of Mammon and creating a just welfare society based on solidarity and the social welfare of others. The mystic must increase their libraries' size, be open, and welcome conversation in the marketplace.

SEVEN

Humans' greed looks upon this world, its creatures, and its objects as commodities for use and abuse. As a result, there is much disregard for others, other beings, and the Earth. A new understanding of God and oneness with other animals can lead to a caring, healthy relational spirituality grounded in solidarity, mindfulness, and compassion.

Of Squirrels and Other Things

On my usual morning walk, a squirrel beside herself confronted me. The squirrel, immensely agitated, chattered and screeched, darted halfway up the tree, then ran down to the ground. It squatted on its hind legs and loudly shouted and hissed at me. The squirrel repeated this behavior several times. I stood rooted to the spot, somewhat scared and confused. Finally, it dawned on me that the flustered squirrel was angrily complaining about what had happened the night before.

For several hours the previous night, the neighbor across the road put on a mindless, selfish, illegal, personal light and sound show of patriotism in celebration of American Independence Day. The squirrel, who held citizenship only in God's heaven, did not keep this celebration. The squirrel and her family must have been traumatized by the offensive smell of burning gunpowder and the exploding surround of firecrackers, bursting, blinding, and lighting the street and sky. It was a warzone. I began to interpret the squirrel's angry chattering as tongue-speech and her hissing as cussing at me in-between the screeches and hisses. I must admit that I felt responsible for what happened. After all, I was created human and charged with the task of being God's steward over God's "lesser" creatures and habitat.

I tried to comfort this beautiful, gray North American squirrel speaking for her civil liberties and defending her space and dignity as God's unique creature. She made a strong case for her young family's welfare. I agreed with her that my neighbor's behavior was a senseless, inconsiderate act. I empathized, acknowledging that she and her children suffered the loss of sleep and trauma. I tried to console her by explaining that I, too, was a victim the night before. I also endured the invasion of privacy and loss of the sleep of justice. Eventually, the squirrel left, muttering that all humans are alike, as she ascended to be with her family nesting near the pinnacle of the tall oak tree. I wished I could have done more for this fellow divine creature and her beloved family.

On the 4th of July, more pets go missing in the USA than on any other day of the year. There is no accurate tally of the many creatures that suffer trauma or die from insensitive celebrations using fireworks. My disgust turned to critique capitalism and its investment and partnership with technology to change the earth's base elements in toys that shock and awe God's creatures. Insensitivity and cruelty to animals indicate an underlying psychological disorder in humans. Left unattended translates into brutal acts towards all sentient beings and the Earth's destruction.

Desperately, for the sake of morality alone, we need an understanding that brings this world, its creatures, and God into an intimate community of healthy relationships. For this to happen, there must be a new Cosmology-Theology grounded in the Science of the day. Humans have a significant role in dissolving the traditional, outdated ideology that distances God from creation. This world must become sacred again for the sake of healthy relationships and the preservation of God's earthly dwelling place and our eternal home. We have labored in thought using dualist philosophy that separated God from creation for too long, separating corrupt from profane. This disingenuous conceptual separation of God from God's beloved creation has become big business. God's world, creatures, rivers, mountains, trees, and the ground are up for sale for filthy lucre. Global Capitalism produces global abuse of the earth and exploitation. Even life is not sacred.

The prescientific old Cosmology-Theology of the Bible presents God seated on *his* throne, and Jesus beneath God, with heaven, and hell set below in their fixed places. The belief that Creation is corrupt, not eternal, has not worked out well for God's "lesser" creatures and the natural world. This low view of Creation does not work well even for humans today. We need a new Cosmology and Theology aligned with Modern Science to transform humans into moral beings who will save this planet and its animals.

Before the Copernican Revolution, traditional beliefs placed the Earth and humans at a small solar system center. In the post-Copernicus and Galileo era, Scientists discovered in the vastness of space an ever-expanding Universe. Also, the planet we live on is insignificant, and the earth is no longer the center of the solar system. Our world is a tiny part of a vast Universe, coexisting in an expanding ecosystem of galaxies, stars, planets, and other objects. Sparse Scientific knowledge of the Universe in which we live supported the view that Man is the highest creature at the center of the Universe. The discovery of other galaxies like ours raises the odds that life does exist elsewhere, that man may not be the highest form of species. The Book of Proverbs ridicules man as a sluggard and directs him to the ant for wisdom.

Proud, arrogant humans can regain lost humility and retrieve a healthy perspective of self by learning this universe's vastness. Learning about

Cosmology, Theology, and Astronomy humbles, heals, and shapes moral character.

One can begin by asking how many galaxies are there in the Universe? Scientists use various wavelengths and intensities of a wide range of electromagnetic signals to count the number of galaxies. The number of galaxies has risen to approximately 2.0 trillion galaxies. In each universe, there are between 100 and 200 billion stars. Around each star, there is a solar system. There are between 10 to 100 billion solar systems, which are similar to ours in each galaxy. The Universe continues to expand. One hundred fifty billion new stars are born per year in the entire Universe. We can extrapolate that since the birth of the Universe, solar systems similar to ours appear every 0.0002 seconds. Humility produces knowledge. Applied knowledge comes from the practical wisdom that survival depends on the concept of community or solidarity- healthy relationships with the natural world and sentient creatures such as humans and squirrels.

Humans need an existential experience of God in creation, the God who is as big as the expanding universe, if not larger. Traditional Religion can provide the key, the segway, a portal for encountering Divine presence in this Universe. However, God works in individual lives. Human history depends on sacrifice or kenosis- spiritual self-emptying of egoist conceptual baggage. The God within Creation, who is essentially love, is *Christ,* God's spirit or soul. Humans aware of this God live in this world bathed in love.

In the Book of Genesis, God creates by the *logos,* the Word, or Spirit. Creation is the work of God's outpouring, the Christ. Traditional Christianity confuses the word *Christ* as Jesus's last name. In both the Hebrew and Greek Scriptures. Christ is God, present at the event of Creation, 13.8 billion years ago, long before the birth of the man Jesus of Nazareth. Jesus, the man, is Christ's embodiment or incarnation manifested in time. Jesus is not *just* God, and not *only* human but is God and human together. We, too, are Christ's embodiment in this world, and so is the rest of the physical universe. A personal God is sentimental, small, and clannish. A personal God is conceptual and never leaves the confines of ideology and philosophy. Putting Jesus and Christ together gives us God, who is both personal and global. Jesus delivers the map for the individual life here and now, and Christ is God's universal plan for all people, time, and space. Christ puts the locus of God, the Soul of God, within all things created. With Christ in our innermost being, the soul, we can mirror God's love to others, other creatures, and the world. Without God's spirit of love, Christians cannot love like Christ.

We live in a sacred universe, and God demands respect, compassion, and love for God's creative handiwork. For this godly work, we need a theology of the Cosmos that relies on the best science of the day so that the world can turn sacred again and squirrels find fairness and the peace of all things. The acknowledgment of intrinsic value, beauty, and soul in all creation, elements, plants, and animals is contrary to most Christians' conceptual beliefs. Humans have proved selfish, limiting God's salvation and activity mainly to human beings, thinking there was not enough God to go around. In this theology of scarcity, stinginess, or tight-fistedness, humans divide the Universe into the sacred and profane, disingenuously respecting and disrespecting arbitrarily. Human selfishness is at the basis of the exploitation of God's earthly dwelling place for personal gain. God is greater than the Universe and is in all created things. There is a distinction between *pantheism* and *panentheism*- God *is* everything, and God *is in* everything. Panentheism is not pantheism. Awareness of God's presence in creation and God's need for the natural world awaken the human soul's spiritual attributes of kindness and compassion.

The incarnation, God, becoming Jesus in John's gospel, is a much broader event than that proposed by traditional beliefs. God embodies *all flesh-* other humans, mountains, a blade of grass, birds, and squirrels. When God's spirit (soul) inhabits matter, then matter becomes a holy thing. When we respect all things as sacred, we appreciate, delight, and love God in all things. In a healthy religion, God, in all things, is the focus of worship. The acknowledgment that everything created possesses Christ- God's soul- leads to a relationship known as "oneness" or solidarity and translates as loving respect for the other. The soul meeting with the soul in the other is love.

Systemic disregard and disrespect for the world are destroying God's creatures and the environment. Democracy, representative rule, and capitalism, two sacred Western Civilization institutions, sow freely to the wind, reaping a global harvest of rapacious corruption. Globalization, the new form of the pandemic virus of Colonialism, continues to wreak havoc in the masses' lives, maiming and killing all God's creatures and turning the earth into lifeless carbon. In a Global Capitalist world, the epicenter of Corporate Colonial Greed patriotically celebrates its wealthy lifestyle. In the more significant part of the colonized planet, the masses gather in graveyards, surrounded by ghostly ancestors, moaning the litany of the lament of victimhood, sickness, death, and loss incessantly.

The global chorus of voices shouting the people's loss of sacred land and destruction of Earth, God's holy dwelling place, is lost on disingenuous deaf deceitful jingoistic hearts rationalizing destructive progress and development despite the loss of countless lives, young and old. In the USA, native Americans still beat the drum and sing the lyrics of heavenly ancestors longing to rest in the native land alongside their living descendants. They march in protest alongside the living for the sake of preservation of sacred ancestral spaces. Their drumbeats call for the cessation- of rape and pollution of the sacred land, mining by fracking, and the unsteady flow of oil pipelines.

In South Africa, natives still are landless, for no one wants to face reparation after Colonialism. The ANC leadership, beginning with Mandela, has successively mortgaged South Africa's land and national assets to Capitalist Corporations and Private Companies. The people mass in the makeshift tin and cardboard shacks outside big cities and industrial parks, begging for survival as chattel labor. Generally, out of sight of Corporations, the abused masses, the wealthy, and the middle-class appear as ghostly essential services as servants. The super-rich and middle-class disingenuously blame the poor for their poverty, vigorously defending the "sacred" systems and structures, and affluent lifestyles. efending the "sacred" systems Middle-class, brilliant economists propose palliative and ameliorative programs of assistance for the impoverished masses. Unfortunately, research for the poor's response and needs does not consider the social, political, and economic context. Most liberal responses are inadequate, efficient, not sufficient. There is muted silence for the demise or dismantling of the system of Capitalism. The wealthy and middle-class rest peacefully, knowing that the machines of evil schemes and structures remain intact for tomorrow's profit.

In India, in cahoots with the government, Capitalist developers displace farmers, forcefully removing them off their land and livelihood using institutional violence. Developers destroy homes and communities, forever changing the voiceless lives in the name of destructive development and progress. In an instant, fertile soil lies bare and barren by the damming and changing rivers' flow. The poor farmers receive little or no compensation for lost land. The farmers' suicide rate in India ranges between 1.4 and 1.8% per 100,000 total population over ten years. In 2018, the average was more than ten suicides daily. Ecologically, developers in bed with governments lay the earth to waste for its valuable minerals. Dams cause flooding, waterlogging, pollution of the water, and the spread of disease. The reality is that dams have a shelf life. They serve out their monetary value as soon as they fill with silt. The illiterate, poor, rural folk retreat in droves to the big cities for survival, sleeping on sidewalks. The police shoot and kill people for urinating and defecating in public. Capitalism robs the poor and destroys livelihood and lives in India.

In the USA, the epicenter of Global Capitalism, the Census Bureau in 2018 found 38.1 million people are poor. Approximately 8.5%, 27.5 million people went without health care. The USA is a country that spends .53 cents on the dollar on defense. Martin Luther King, Jr., in 1968, addressing sanitation workers in Memphis, Tennessee, said that America is the wealthiest country in the world and pays its people starvation wages. From the Poor People's Campaign in the USA, Dr. William Barber demands a reconstruction of everything by bringing attention to the widespread plight of poverty and inequality. He hopes to change the country's moral narrative and build political power to end the injustice of poverty. One cannot remain soulless in the face of the souls who suffer the effects of Global Capitalism.

Only a new Cosmology-Theology that respects the New Science will translate into healthy relationships with Christ, the God in creation, the world, and other creatures. The universe we live in is a community of subjects, not commodities for sale, bonded by oneness or solidarity. This theological realization alone should birth our humanity and energize compassion deep within the human soul, all creatures, and God's and our earthly home. The new Cosmology -Theology, the encounter with God's spirit, the Christ in Creation, awareness of solidarity with everything, translates into a spirituality of loving relationships and care for all sentient beings and the world.

Next time, there will be no senseless, mindless shock and awe sound and light show on my street to celebrate patriotic days on the secular calendar. Instead, there will be a protest march with placards in hand the night before any loud holiday. I am confident with a slight organizing effort; the grassroots protest will include several neighbors and squirrels bearing placards. Emblazoned on the posters will be the only relevant verse of the hymn. *All Things Bright and Beautiful.*

> All things bright and beautiful,
> All creatures, great and small,
> All things wise and wonderful,
> The Lord God made them all.

EIGHT

In the early 1900s, the Protestant Church in the USA experienced a revival of faith. Several conferences agreed on the gospel's fundamentals-basic beliefs that became non-negotiable for the believer's salvation. However, the traditional understanding of the centrality of Jesus for the work of salvation dominated Christian thought. The thinking of the centrality of Jesus pushed God away from direct involvement in people's personal lives and the human condition. This sermon raises questions about the text that fundamentalist believers use as a driving thrust to grow the church numerically, challenge, and convert others. It also proposes that God's love in Jesus must and still be at the center of the strategy to win the hearts of all, regardless of cultural differences.

The prophets criticized those who practiced the outward forms of religion that satisfied the Ego. This sermon examines the purpose of the external practice of the ritual act of Baptism. It emphasizes that baptism is the initiation into a life lived in union with God in liminal space. In baptism, Ego is humiliated, and God's presence kindles the relationship for transformation. Baptism can be the portal to living in that liminal space where one encounters God's spirit.

The Baptism of Jesus

In the third chapter of Matthew's gospel, Jesus presents himself to the wilderness preacher, his cousin John, for the baptism for repentance, confession of sins, and preparation for the coming kingdom of God. Jesus's presentation to John for baptism raises many questions about why Jesus needed John's baptism and the meaning and significance of baptism in later Church tradition.

In Matthew's gospel, John's baptism raises questions about faith as trust in beliefs and faith as trust in God through a relationship with creation. Faith understood as trust in ideas, dogma, and doctrine can only exist in a constructed dualist worldview where God lives in another realm separated from this world. Instead, faith is understood as relational trust in God's presence in creation and recognizes that God is present in everything.

Matthew's gospel, one of the three synoptic gospels, is placed first in the Bible, even though Matthew wrote his gospel after Mark. According to New Testament scholars, Mark wrote the first gospel for a mainly Jewish audience, telling them their long-awaited Messiah had come. Matthew's gospel makes many references to the Hebrew Scriptures that spoke of the birth of the Messiah. Reading Matthew's gospel with Greek and Roman philosophical spectacles leads to misunderstanding his message and theoretical speculations.

What did Jews understand about the Messiah? Messiah in Jewish culture meant the "anointed one," the king from the house of David. The Messiah would deliver the people from their Roman oppressors. When the Scribes turned up to receive John's baptism, John prohibited them. He saw these officials as hypocrites who practiced a religion's externals based on fear, prejudice, and competition with others. John's baptism required the fruit of repentance, the turning around from the Sin of apostasy to live in union with God. John had grown weary with religion that practiced the outward forms while denying its inner power. John, the mystic prophet, lived in the wild places, off the grid, dressed in camel's hair, eating locusts and honey. He knew the meditative peace of natural things found only in the in-between prayer space where divinity embraced the weary anguished soul. John vigorously challenged the Scribes with tough love, even resorting to name-calling. For John, the fruit of repentance was the spirituality of self-realization in God through emptying the false self, the Ego. In this liminal space, the soul encounters Christ, the blueprint of the God of Love known by different names, in creation.

GOD HAPPENS

In the dark discard of the slain dress of the habit of Ego
In the naked kiss of earthy embrace
God happens.
Genesis
Evolution
Worldly humanity births Essence
Known by names of healing
Agape'
Kindness
Compassion
Justice with joy kisses righteousness
Peace rolls down like a River

John's heart reached out to the Scribes with compassion to save them from the Ego's vain creations of misguided religion. He was a Jew steeped in the mystic tradition of the prophets. He longed for the day when a Messiah would come from the royal house of David, be anointed as king, and rescue God's nation from the chains of Imperialism, and the Sin of apostasy. John stood within the prophetic tradition that discerned God's people as playing the whore, consorting with egotist Imperialism, and energizing egoistic religious practices and beliefs. John believed that his baptism would rescue God's beloved from the Sin of apostasy and look forward with expectation for the Messiah's arrival. The Messiah would baptize with fire, dissolve Ego's hold on the mind, and restore in their hearts that faith understood as a relationship with God, God in others, and God in the natural world. This restoration of faith understood as a personal relationship with God, John knew, would rekindle the flame of the God of love in the soul.

In Matthew's gospel, Jesus, the Galilean mystic preacher, presents to John for John's water baptism. He did not need to repent of the Ego's sin of apostasy. Nor did Jesus need to reconnect with God. As a mystic, he had transcended the lower levels of the primitive egoist conceptual faith. Jesus was not interested in energizing belief systems, confirming opinions, and blindly adhering to institutional religious doctrine. Jesus already achieved the highest stage of relational faith that lived in the kingdom of God. In the kingdom of God, the liminal space of authentic prayer, God's spirit burns away Ego's primitive animalistic consciousness with compassionate love. The Ego dissolves in the essence of love. The true self emerges like a butterfly, self-realized in God, the Ultimate Reality.

When Jesus presented himself to John, Jesus had already cleared the path to God. Jesus had achieved the spiritual state of the union in God. Jesus was already there where the Baptist wanted people to be. Jesus had already reached that level of a faith relationship, the evolutionary perfection of the human species, measured nothing less than the full stature of the Christ of unconditional, sacrificial love. Jesus was already in his perfect state of creation. His soul mirrored the image and likeness of God to all that passed his way.

John, when he saw his cousin at the river, was confused and surprised. John tried hard to prevent Jesus, but Jesus insisted, saying that the baptism was to fulfill all righteousness. John's baptism was an integral step toward a right relationship with God and God in others. Jesus did not know his cousin John well. John's baptism showed that righteousness connected with John by visiting and identifying with John and John's message. Matthew, the evangelist, speaks through John, saying John used water baptism to turn people in God's direction. Jesus's baptism of fire introduced people into the transforming life where one lives continually in God.

Church tradition is guilty of reading back into the primitive gospel, 2000 years of egoist beliefs, doctrines, and dogma. Scholars have complained that the dogmatic faith is essentially an adaptation of Christianity to the values and requirements of Greek and Roman culture, initially, the Imperial establishment's demand. Traditional beliefs of baptism have deviated from the message of the Jesus of the early gospels. Jesus's message centered primarily on corralling the sheep through the gate into the kingdom where God and love abounds. This love was powerful enough to influence and subdue the Ego, fill the heart with unconditional love, and change the stubborn will to work for change in the corrupt human condition.

The verse Matthew 28:19 is a later insertion into the original gospel written between 80A.D and 90A.D. This insertion steered the direction of Jesus's spiritual message away from the necessary dissolution of the Ego for life in God's kingdom. The later addition of the text to Matthew's gospel empowered the church to align with the Empire's program of colonizing and subjugating nations through the rite of baptism in the name of the conceptual Trinity. Today, this verse validates the Great Commission and empowers Christians to colonize the world with egoist institutional religion. This toxic practice of doctrine before spirituality destroys relationships and peace in the world. Disingenuous institutional religion focuses on seating people in the pews rather than sending people out with God's unconditional love. Jesus's baptism of fire is the baptism into the crucible of God's love for the vocation of love in the world.

In Matthew's gospel, John validly criticizes egoist institutional religion. Those who represent hypocrisy, division, and the deprivation of God's grace in the marketplace of faith. Understanding baptism to mean merely belonging produces the bitter fruit of keeping the outward forms while denying the inner power of love for all in the gospel of Jesus. John refused baptism to the high officials of religion, representatives of their constituency. He required the condition of bearing the fruit of repentance. John still stands today at the proverbial river crying out in the wilderness, making the same altar call. He requests the same show of remorse from all the baptized and repentance of egoist religion's baptism. John's baptism is the only door that leads to Jesus' baptism, the baptism of fire for life in union with God, to mirror the blueprint of the Christ in creation.

What does Baptism mean in these last days of extreme crisis?

Pandemic crises reveal the Ego's civilization's vulnerability. We live in an era obsessively entangled with flawed systems, structures, institutions, ideologies, and theologies. In disgust, the crowds, mainly the youth, take to the streets in protest, marching, looting, and burning down the proud, arrogant symbols of disrespect and disregard for the powerless and voiceless. The super-rich and middle-class panic and respond liberally, focusing foolishly on the symptoms while disregarding the systems. Simultaneously, the cause, the Ego, sits unnoticed in the center of the room. The rich and middle-class respond with liberal palliatives, which serve to preserve the status quo. Chom Noamsky's definition: *"liberal" in the intellectual culture means highly conformist to power but mildly critical.*

Jesus presented himself for baptism at the start of his mandated mission in the world of crisis. Ego's world and its systems and structures were toppling around him. Jesus knew Ego's work in the world and the soul. He was aware that that Ego sat smugly in the living room. Ego's job is always cosmetic reform, illusionary rescue, and preservation of the status quo. Jesus taught the loss of Ego, the effective vaccine, the ultimate cure for the subdued soul, and the flawed human condition of systems and structures.

After losing Ego's fear in the upper room, the early way of Jesus's movement, filled with the courage of God's spirit of love, initiated alternative organic, grassroots communities. These communities were non-hierarchical, unincorporated, organic, bottom-up, and focused on the powerless poor. The organic movement focused on the poor, vulnerable, and voiceless material needs based on solidarity. But, unfortunately, the way of life of the baptized, centered solely on the individual's psycho-spiritual health, eventually added strength to the corrupt program of the Roman Empire.

In pandemic crises, Baptism positively serves as the portal to the new way of dying and being in the world, the life of solidarity with others, and the collective empowerment of organic movements to be salt and light in the tasteless, lifeless dark world.

NINE

Anguish, pain, and suffering drives one to ask deep questions about God and life. In extreme personal trauma, the question of why God remains distant is uppermost in the troubled mind. In the moment of great suffering, the anxious mind finds it hard to focus on the God present in creation. Ego succeeds in convincing the victim that God may be the cause of suffering or does not exist. Times of deep sorrow, anguish, pain, and death can also be the breakthrough into God's presence. Many who have endured have experienced hope, new meaning, and purpose for life. Even when something dies, something new is born. Global suffering and death shine the spotlight on civilization's weakest links. Old systems and structures must make way for God's way of love. One cannot enter into the new way of living with old baggage. God requires new wineskins for a new wine.

Death and Resurrection in the Context of Pandemic Crises

World War II (1942-1945) was the pandemic virus of the day. This virus spread its pain, loss, suffering, and death worldwide from its German hotspot. Hitler, the leader of Germany, wanted to establish himself as the dictator of the world. His egoist disoriented desires aimed at creating *"a right side up"* totalitarian State controlled by rigid rules of *"ought"* and *"ought not."* In 1949, when the world was still reeling from the aftermath of the Second World War, Disney produced an animated musical film based on the children's classic *Alice in Wonderland.* The film was timely. The world had not yet rallied fully from the pain, suffering, and death of the war. Disney simply aimed to entertain, educate, and provide some answers to questions still swirling in people's shell-shocked heads. He produced the film based on Lewis Carroll's children's classic. Disney hoped to entertain children and simultaneously motivate adults to participate in a paradigm shift of thinking that would never repeat such a ghastly human-made tragedy in the world.

In the film, Disney socially analyses what had gone dreadfully wrong with the world and courageously proposes a radical possibility to make things right again. Using dualistic thought, Disney contrasts the contrived egoist world with the world of the free spirit. Thus, he provides an insightful social scientific analysis of the past world and his hopes for the future world. Disney embeds a revolutionary proposal in the lyrics in the song Upside Down that appears as a frivolous ditty. We witness the dysfunctional world as merely the collective Ego drama acting out on the perceived stage of form and time. Extreme times demand extreme solutions. Listen to the words of the song *Upside Down,* sung by Alice.

> *I'm upside down; I'm upside down. At last, I'm having my way.*
> *The rules for what I ought, and ought not to, are unimportant*
> *today. Life was slow when low was low and high was always high,*
> *Till I found the roof on the ground, the floor in the sky. I'm upside*
> *down and downside up. As far as I can foresee, the most incredible*
> *Wonderland will be.* (Sol Kaplan and Edward Eliscu)

The lawful world of "ought" and "ought not" sucks the life breath out of everything. On the other hand, the creative spirit world is full of life, love, vibrancy, enthusiasm, and goodness. Ego's rules, words, and ideas dissolve into a morally higher realized consciousness in the world of the ultimate reality. The upside-down Wonderland symbolizes the realm of higher consciousness or ultimate reality where hope springs eternal in the face of misery.

Alice falls down the rabbit hole, lands on her head, and experiences the "upside-down" world. She discovers that everything in this Wonderland to the eyes that cannot see is topsy-turvy. What was impossible in the prior regimented rigid egoist world of inflexible rules is now possible in Wonderland's upside-down. Life is a curious explosion of fun, an incredible discovery of slipping and sliding down adventurous paths that lead to fun-filled parties and intriguing meetings with odd people. There is never a dull movement in this upside-down Wonderland with upside-down rules. The old order of death with the right-side-up laws has passed away, and the new has arrived.

Falling down the rabbit hole is the metaphor for death and dying. The way of death is the portal, the gateway to the new way of living in Wonderland. Wonderland is not a place in some alternate universe but is the realm at hand. Alice's experience takes place in a world where everything is possible. One enters this higher state of spiritual consciousness by dying to the world of right-side-up rules of the ought's and ought not. When Alice falls down the rabbit hole, she experiences a new way of living-resurrection, awakening, or enlightenment.

In natural religion and the Christian tradition, death is the gateway to new life, resurrection, or awakening. In the Christian tradition, Easter celebrates new life, transformation, revival, and renewal. Oddly, the Christian Easter symbol is the resurrected rabbit, bursting out of the dark cave of death, free to live again in this world. In Wonderland, Lewis Carroll's Alice is about spiritually dying to the self and rising to the new way of living with the world's upside rule. The upside rule in the world is love. At Easter, those prepared for initiation in the Christian religion go down into the water with God's spiritual presence, mimicking the message of Jesus's spiritual death. The newly baptized come out of the water revived by the God of love who raised Jesus from death. God's spirit, Christ, resides with the baptized for the new loving way of living in the Kingdom of God in this world. The Kingdom of God is the liminal space we find ourselves in when death, loss, and suffering come our way. It is the place of waiting, the home of prayer, where infinite possibilities arrive with the God of the dawn. The prophet Isaiah said: *Those that wait shall renew their strength, and they shall rise with wings of eagles. They will run and not grow weary. They will walk and not faint.* In the liminal space, egoist belief systems, firmly held uninformed opinions, and flawed ecclesiastical doctrines dissolve into God's higher essential consciousness of unconditional love. This contemplative spiritual path transcends egoist ideas, beliefs, and theories that parade as absolute truth. Ego's perception of the world is always the truth.

Pandemic viruses such as pestilence, disease, and wars bring death, destruction, and anguish. They are also a mixed blessing, serving us a plate of bitter herbs while being teachers simultaneously. Weirdly, pandemic viruses reveal the cracks in the bedrock of civilization, including religion. They shed light on personal lives, uncovering the layers of Ego that obscure our souls and prevent us from seeing the wisdom of living spiritually. They also shed light on the flawed systems and structures that serve the collective Ego's control, domination, and exploitation program. How should one view personal, national, or global disasters? Disasters reveal the fault lines in the systems and networks' egoist mind, society, and egoist structures. The world exists by deadly rules that kill the soul and stubbornly resist God's only law of love for others. Pandemic viruses of wars, pestilence, and disease provide an opportunity to listen to the God of love, who spotlight the alienated and those who suffer in the human condition.

The Lord Jesus, the embodiment of God's spirit, the Christ, preached in parables the less-traveled path of self-awareness, awareness of the planet, and self-realization in the God of Love. The early church lost its way when it laid aside Jesus, the cornerstone, his way of living immersed in God's spirit, and his message of unconditional love. Jesus hoped to set fire to the world with the right-side-up structures that lacked God's love. Unfortunately, he did not live to see the day when his love movement helped build God's kingdom on the ashes of the toppled Empire.

Pandemics turn Ego's sacred and secular structures and systems on its head. One cannot deny the intense anxiety, panic, and suffering that abounds when global disasters strike the world. The Ego desperately uses suffering to convince our minds that God remains far from us. We are one in God, and God is one with us. God will never leave us or forsake us. Many interpret disasters as God's signs of God's anger with humanity. This belief of an angry, vengeful God came from the Medieval era. The art from this period focuses on humanity's sinful nature and an angry God requiring payment for sins. There is no wrath in the God of love who, in Jesus, showed us the way to God's kingdom of love. Julian of Norwich, a mystic during the Medieval plague, assured everyone that all would be well, and everything would be well. She also understood that Sin, an illusion had no substance. Pain caused by Sin has material content. Through the hard times of illness, suffering, violence, and war, Julian of Norwich manifested a life filled with peace that comes through contemplative prayer.

Jesus taught the way of death and released the Ego's sturdy grip on the mind and its irresistible obsession with creating and maintaining flawed ideas, institutional systems, and structures. The first step towards healing and wellness is the admission that there is an ego. The second step is embracing the message of Jesus to leave the self behind. The third step is living in liminal space, the in-between realm, in contemplative prayer. In this space, the God of unconditional love dwells. The shadows of death in Ego's world encounter the light of love, new life, and hope. The dawning light transforms everything. Love emerges to reign supreme again in this world.

Death and Resurrection are the two sides of the same coin. Alice went down the rabbit hole and found a new way of life with others. Jesus died and rose again to a new life in God's kingdom of love. Death in the kingdom of God kisses the life-giving lips of Resurrection.

TEN

This sermon focuses on what Paul saw as the gospel's central message of the man Jesus of Nazareth. Paul's constant reflection on the cross revealed the mystery of God's saving love for him and the world. In his continuous battle with the intellectuals of his day, Paul preached the cross of Christ, using no wisdom from the philosophy that rationalized belief in a God separated from the human condition. Paul's testimony was that the cross of Christ, the symbol of God's saving love, was powerful enough to save him from his sin of separation from God's way of love. This power of Christ's love on the cross also raised Jesus from death.

The Cross of Christ

Paul's conversion experience on the Damascus Road radically changed his outlook towards those tribal Jewish religions considered outcasts. Paul, a Jew, followed his Jewish faith to the extent that he was willing to kill others who believed differently. He was so devoted that he obtained letters from religious authority to travel to Damascus to persecute those in Jesus's movement. On the road to Damascus, Paul had a mysterious experience that led to his dramatic conversion. During a storm, the horse, spooked by a lightning strike, threw Paul to the ground. Paul saw a vision where he heard the resurrected Jesus Christ speak to him, concerned about why Paul persecuted him by hurting his followers.

Paul was a hater of the man Jesus and his message. God reached out in Love to Paul and rescued him from the prison of the illusions of egoist religious hatred, fears, bigotry, and violence. Paul's conversion experience was a momentary liminal experience. God reached Paul in his darkest hour, calmed the storms within his soul, and replaced in his mind Ego's institutional transactional love for God's unconditional love. In the future, Paul looked at others- Athenians in the Geek religion and Jesus followers with empathy, compassion, and unconditional love. Paul lived in the assurance that: *In God, we live, move, and have our being.* Paul knew this God as the Christ who raised Jesus from the dead. In his conversion, Paul's learned that God is the God of immense love and directly identifies with humanity's dilemma and suffering. Christ rescued Paul from his tremendous guilt. Reflecting on Paul's experience, we gain insight into the nature of Christ, who changed Paul, who believed himself of no worth, to be of tremendous value, even for others.

Paul superseded all his fellow apostles' work combined and established churches in Syria, Turkey, Greece, and Rome as an apostle. Possibly, he was the most prolific writer of all his colleagues. Only his works survived the scrutiny of the Canon committee. Thirteen of his letters to his churches occupy a prominent presence in the New Testament Canon. The Book of Acts, the second volume of Luke's gospel, is the biography of Paul of Tarsus in Syria. Luke, a great fan of Paul, promoted Paul as superseding Jesus's sufferings to spread the gospel of Jesus. Paul's writings devote much to his experience of God's measureless mysterious unconditional inclusive Love and practical wisdom for the corrupt human condition. For Paul, the cross was the ultimate symbol of God's powerful love shown in mercy and forgiveness. The same power of God that saved Jesus from humanity's ultimate enemy called death, Paul experienced the authority for salvation and transformation for a new way of being in the world.

Paul, like any church planter or pastor, had problems with the congregations he planted. As soon as Paul left to plant another church, Ego quickly raised its ugly head, sowing seeds of fear, distrust, and meanness among the people. Intellectual, Greek philosophical disagreements caused conflicts, and relationships soured. The freedom, love, and unity they experienced as God's spirit dissipated into divisive power struggles. The Church in Corinth took up much of Paul's attention and energy. Paul, who showed the Corinthian church love rather than fear, was personally attacked by the corporate Ego.

Paul wrote four love letters to his church in Corinth, Greece. The choice of writing rather than visiting indicated how dangerous the situation was in the congregation. The problems in this Greek Corinthian church ran so deep, cutting beyond flesh and bone, affecting the soul, spiritual life, public worship, private prayer, and fellowship. The community fractured into various divisions, and relationships with Paul became strained and aloof. They refused to regard Paul as equal to the other apostles and discredited his status among them. Paul, in their opinion, had no authority over them as an apostle. The basis of their argument was that Paul did not have the essential credential of seeing or knowing Jesus personally. They discounted Paul's visionary experience on the Damascus Road as a qualifying credential for apostleship. The people were so angry that Paul, for his safety, refused to meet face-to-face and resorted to writing letters. Paul discerned a host of problems in the Church at Corinth that included Greek cultural and philosophical influence, enthusiastic disordered worship, and misuse of the spiritual gifts.

Corinth was a Greek port city. The kind of worship service in the Greek temples crept into Paul's church in Corinth. Worship in the Greek temples sensually satisfied the individual, did not build community, was competitive, and prominently featured speaking in tongues. In his usual diplomatic style, Paul affirmed the church's worship experience. Still, he critiqued them for not including the God of Love for ordered worship and healthy relationships. More seriously, the Corinthians separated the gifts of God from God the giver, turning them into idols that competed for first place in worship services. Paul reminded them that God was a God of order and required an ordered inclusive, participatory liturgy aimed at unity with God in each other. He encouraged them to distinguish between the higher gifts and the lower gifts. The higher gifts of intuitive wisdom, knowledge, faith, healing, miracles, prophecy, and tongues' discernment when people spoke in tongues helped sustain community life. Like tongue-speaking, the lower gifts served a minimal purpose in inspiring communal love and worship. The Corinthian church began to present pathological symptoms that manifested a disconnect between God and God's love. The Corinthians began to use the semblance of God's gifts without the presence of God's Spirit of love. The church reduced the spiritual gifts of God into talents that flattered the egoist personality.

The disconnect from God's spiritual presence turns the gifts into idols of worship and money. Paul was concerned that God's love was not present in the Corinthian worship experience. He intuitively knew this because where there is God, there is love. God's spirit of love, the Christ. One discerns the Christ of love in others by the fruits of love, joy, peace, forbearance, kindness, goodness, faithfulness, and self-control. Instead, Corinthian worship displayed the Ego and ego's egoistic aspirations for power, control, and competition.

Paul had noticed that Greek culture, philosophy, and exuberant liturgy of worship, including tongue-speaking prominence, crept into the Corinthian worship experience. The Greek philosophy of dualism, the separation of God from the world, led the Corinthian church to separate the giver from the gifts, especially during worship meetings. Paul drew on the wisdom given to him in his Damascus Road spiritual experience of the God in Christ. The latter reaches out and always encourages love.

Paul always apologized for the God of unconditional love when others preached an intellectual faith based on reason. For Paul, flawed rational beliefs posed a danger, a stumbling block to the spiritual pathway of living in God's presence for evolutionary growth into God's image and likeness. Spirituality for Paul was intentional, disciplined learning, awareness, and exploration that transcended mental concepts. Paul criticized faith based on Greek dualist philosophy that relegated God to a place beyond this world and outside human experience.

Spirituality, for Paul, transcended mental concepts and living based on cause and effect, rewards, and punishments. Paul writes in Colossians: *Beware that any man spoils you through philosophy and vain deceit, after the tradition of men, after the rudiments of the world, and not of Christ.* Christ, for Paul, was the God of love he had encountered in his epiphany on the Damascus Road. After his conversion, Paul used the Cross of Christ to represent the height, depth, breadth, and width of God's immeasurable transforming love. Paul saw God Christ's saving work of love as a powerful symbol for meaning and purpose. God identified with the human predicament and empowered all humans with love for others. Paul's testimony was that God was not a religious belief based on the rationale of eloquent philosophy. The symbol of the cross of Christ, emptied of all human wisdom, is God's saving power for salvation. Paul wrote: *But God forbid that I should boast except in the cross of our Lord Jesus Christ, by whom the world has been crucified to me, and I to the world.*

For Paul, the Cross of Christ did not connect with Greek ideas of atonement or substitutionary theories; theories developed long after Paul. Paul knew a loving God who saved a wretch like him without the spilling of blood. Paul, who conspired to murder, deserved punishment but received mercy as the unconditional healing love that transformed him. Paul always remembered God as the Christ, who is the spirit of love. Paul's God of love was not an egoist dualist belief of cause and effect, reward and punishment, or retributive justice. The love that Paul encountered on the cross can be a present experience for those who live, move, and live their lives in God.

The cross symbolizes Christ's identification with victims of the corrupt social order. God's unconditional love inclusively extends widely to all of God's children regardless of tribal culture or station in life. God on the cross removes humankind's only Sin, the sin of separation. God focuses on humankind's original goodness in relationships with creation, while the religious institution obsesses on human failures. God is the caring father in the prodigal son story, the parable of God in the human condition saving through the wisdom of love signified by the Cross. God shows up as love at the crossroads of life while society dominates by Ego's fear.

ELEVEN

This sermon defines Sin, fasting, and righteousness and focuses on the fasting, its value, and uses. Healthy religion and practices open the door for encountering God and God's grace that transforms humans into righteous individuals who behave justly and fairly with others. The fast that is pleasing to God removes the only Sin of humans. Removal of Sin unites the believer with God,

Sin, Fasting, and Righteousness

Pursuing religious practices without mindfulness of the present God and others and the planet does not reach the goal of union with God and the attainment of transformative power for self, society, and world. Healthy religious rituals can serve as the intermediary practices that lead to a direct encounter with God in the creation, opening the conduit of grace. But if union with God is not the believer's intent, religion, and its accruals such as fasting lead to a cul-de-sac. The Hebrew prophetic writings often warned those who fast to pay careful attention to God's fasting guidelines. In Isaiah, chapter 58, the prophet details God's requirements for fasting, turning the worshipers' pious upward gaze downwards and sideways.

Religion constructs steps that help raise the sin-ridden believer's climb upwards to God's imaginary heavenly abode beyond the skies. The confident priest guides the erring sinner, leading him to the ziggurat's pinnacle with orthodox beliefs, rituals, and spiritual practices. All through the journey upwards, God hides safely in heaven. The prophet performs the opposite role of the priest. The prophet knows God personally as an inner, immanent presence. The prophet, like God, is gravely concerned about self-serving pious religion, oblivious to the cries of those exploited, hurt, and hoping. For the priest, God lives in the sky, socially distant beyond the pinnacle of the Temple. God is as close as one's jugular vein for the prophet, the One who never leaves or forsakes. Humans have only one Sin for the prophet: the illusory egoist belief that God is not an indwelling spirit. The priest only acknowledges humans' failures, unfulfilled human standards or goals as sins, which can be wished away by sacrificing scapegoats. The single message of the prophet is the human response of repentance to live in God, assured of a victorious life. The priest's advice to the failing sinner is leadership training, setting goals, self-control, and measuring one's life against others to feel better. Prophets like Jesus and Paul called the stop of measuring oneself against others. The only human standard was the measurement against the standard of God's unconditional love for others.

A good fast depends on Biblically defining the origin and nature of sin, understanding righteousness, and faith in Hebrew culture. The Hebrew Bible and the Christian Testament differ considerably in context. The Hebrew cultural context is more social and relational. The Roman/Greek culture saw society as an amorphous group of independent individuals. Sin, faith, and righteousness are terms treated differently in these two contexts. The definition of Sin in Jewish culture is a broken relationship with God and others. Also, faith is not just a set of beliefs but a dynamic trust relationship between God and others. A righteous person relates to others justly and fairly. In the Hebrew culture, "sin," "righteousness," and faith are connected and held together in dialogue for deeper meaning. Sin breaks faith or relationships with God and others, thus making one unrighteous. In the Christian tradition, sin, righteousness, and faith are individualized and personalized, having very little to do with just and honest relationships with others.

Healthy Biblical theology disputes any idea that God lives outside of this universe. In the Book of Genesis quoted in John's gospel, God creates and saturates creation as the universal Christ. God's DNA, the Christ, is present in everyone and everything. As the brain evolved and developed in humans, so did Ego consciousness desirous of independence and adventure. Eventually, the Ego deluded the mind into believing the illusion that humans can live separated, unfaithfully, or divorced from God's love in creation. Genesis 1-11 narrates this independent consciousness development over 300 million years in the brain. Throughout this period, the Sin of separation became a natural trait in the genes. Hoarding, scarcity, and competition seeped into Ego's consciousness, destroying the human memory of original goodness of faith, righteousness, knowledge, and understanding of Sin.

The Biblical writers painstakingly remind us of God's love, faithfulness, or righteousness. Humans may lose faith and do unrighteous things, but God keeps faith for God is righteous. There exists an intricate connection between "faith" and "righteous" and "sin" in Biblical Theology. The "righteous" person in the Hebrew Bible, and parts of the Christian Bible, defines the "righteous" person as one who is faithful" and stays in the relationship with God. In the High Priestly Prayer in John's gospel, Jesus prayed and hoped that his learners keep intimately close, faithful, and stay in a relationship with God who lives under the skin. The "righteous," "faithful," "sinless" person remains in a relationship with God, others, other creatures, and the natural world. Faith in Hebrew culture is dynamically personal and relational, with God incarnated in all creation and others. For Hebrews, the transfer of this trust or confidence entirely to religion or beliefs was considered idolatrous. Faith without love deeds to show is dead.

The Christian scriptures and dualist Greek philosophical Church tradition spun the story of God's relationship with humans, translating "Sin," "righteousness," and "faith" differently. The Ego, a late product of the developed human brain, successively convinced humans that God lives divorced from humans and the world. The Ego typically sows seeds of division and deprivation, the foundational pillars of the corrupt human condition globally where social competition and greed dominate.

The Ego's dualism and binary thinking have successfully guided imperial religion to commit the only human Sin of apostasy, the Original Sin. Humans lost original Godness and goodness, God's loving presence, and empowering grace in the illusion of separateness from God. Humans now live apart from God, not personally or corporately strong enough to return and receive strength in God to do good. Many turn to religion, hoping priests will help. Religion only succeeds in raising its followers as far up the steps of faith could lead but nowhere close to the bosom of God for oneness. Dualist theologians warn that oneness with God means death and contamination of the pure God. Religion has proved to be a stumbling block of faith-relationship with God, a deterrent of loving action towards the neighbor, and a significant source of violence. The best of human religion only serves up transactional disingenuous love. For Western theologians like Paul Tillich and the Niebuhrs, faith was much bigger than religion and its ideas. Religion is the cumulative egoist tradition of scripture, narratives, myths, symbols, architecture, music, dance, theologies, creeds, rites, etc. Brain studies reveal that religion and its incremental practices emanate from flawed human minds with Ego that lives apart from God. In Hebrew culture and suppressed mysticism in indigenous cultures, faith is the life lived in God's essential nature of transformative love, knowing human ab-original goodness. God has never left or deserted humans historically.

The universal God is the God of love who longs for a loving relationship. The Church's traditional concept of God only legally requires intellectual assent to religion, laws, and accumulated doctrines and beliefs. Direct encounter and intimate love- relationship with the universal God is not on offer in dualist religion. The academic agreement and trust in doctrinal beliefs idolatrously cannot guarantee a personal relationship with God nor avail experience of grace for knowledge and wisdom for the moral life.

The present apocalypse and the corrupt human condition is a crisis of spirituality. The solution to the human problem lies in a spiritual pathway that leads to a direct encounter with the living God. Religion- the intellectual works of the egoist, vain attempts that miss the mark, feebly deal with human failures, measuring humans against other humans with human standards or goals. The usual proposal of a day's business leadership training cannot cure religion's severe crisis of faith and spirituality. The crisis of spirituality is a crisis of unrighteous relationships, broken relationships with God and neighbor. *There is no one righteous, no not one.*

For Paul, the universal Christ of unconditional love was the standard of measurement. In God's kingdom, acceptable social ethics cannot be the standard of measurement of relationships. Nor can it be the fulfillment of religion and practices. The answer to the social dilemma of corruption and the quest for perfection of a healthy global society lies in attaining oneness with God and keeping faithful and obedient as a child of God of love. John writes:

> *God is love, and all who live in love live in God, and God lives in them. [17]And as we live in God, our love grows perfect.*

We live in a world subjected to egoist illusions of religion, mental ideas, human rituals, and beliefs that capture and keep humans imprisoned in infantile faith. Religion convinces humans to fear and respect the conceptualized distant God absent Father, favorite Son, and tribal Spirit. Religious devotees fear God and fear other humans. God cannot abide living separate from humans and God's dwelling place of creation. The physical structure of humans is inextricably joined with God and is a mixture of God's universal spirit and borrowed dust from the earth. Paul knew this truth when he asked:

> *35Who shall separate us from the love of Christ? Shall tribulation, or distress, or persecution, or famine, or nakedness, or peril, or sword? 36As it is written, For thy sake, we are killed all the day long; we are accounted as sheep for the slaughter. 37Nay, in all these things, we are more than conquerors through him that loved us. 38For I am persuaded, that neither death, nor life, nor angels, nor principalities, nor powers, nor things present, nor things to come, 39Nor height, nor depth, nor any other creature, shall be able to separate us from the love of God, which is in Christ Jesus our Lord.*

God dwells in the inner being of all humans. Humans possess God's DNA of love for God and others. Humans are created eternally righteous, are always connected with God's spirit, and therefore have no Sin. Sin is the egoist illusionary dualist belief that God exists in a separate space and world distant from humans, other creatures, and the Cosmos.

Jesus proposed the only cure for the only human Sin of illusionary belief. He modeled the way, truth, and life that proved an effective cure for the sick mind captivated by Ego's grand illusion. Jesus showed that ordinary humans have God present with them to be extraordinary. By losing Ego and ego's ideas, one can live in original goodness in God, dwelling in that contemplative space of prayer within us and in this world called the Kingdom of God. In the practice of contemplation in liminal space, the righteous person finds grace for transformation, enlightenment, knowledge, wisdom, and love for others. Righteousness and faithful relationships flow when one sacrifices unhealthy cerebral religion and its hollow practices.

Isaiah criticizes egoist religious hypocrisy, misdirection, and meaningless rituals that cleanse the outside of the cup while the inside remains filthy. In his stern message on true fasting, the prophet directs the people to honest relationships such as:

> *losing the bonds of injustice, undoing the thongs of the yoke,*
> *letting the oppressed go free, sharing bread with the hungry,*
> *bringing the homeless into one's home, and covering the naked.*

Extreme pious religion looks up to God and inwards for self-service and selfish interests. Western Christianity, in most respects, is private and hyper-individualistic. Isaiah turns the soul to gaze below and outwards to redress the dysfunctional human condition and the corrupt world.

Paul battled in his entire ministry against egoist conceptual religion based on the Greek philosophy of dualism. He taught nothing that came from human wisdom but the cross of Christ. The cross of Christ was the immeasurable love Paul encountered on the Damascus Road when he was in Sin, separated from God. This love sufficiently dealt with his Sin, pain, and shame and upturned his whole life. Paul lived, moved, and had his being in God the Christ.

Many in this spiritual age find the church tradition's vain rituals failing dismally to bridge the illusory gap, unite worshipers with God, or heal broken relationships with God and others. The outward show of religion preserves Ego's persona, independence, and distance from God for the continuance of a disingenuous life of selfishness, self-interest, blind disregard for the rights of others, and callous treatment of others as enemies and competitors, rather than as kith and kin. The Biblical mystical heroes like Isaiah, Jesus, Paul, and many others, spiritually practiced the fast to feast in the presence of God and God in others. They wanted to be faithful and righteous in all relationships without Ego's Sin, the grand delusion that God is not within us and in creation.

TWELVE

This sermon, written for the celebration of Black History Month, reflects on the poem Lift Every Voice, now the National Anthem for those of color in the USA. The sermon traces African-Americans' history in Africa through the Middle passage and their landing on America's shores. The history of African- Americans is a history of slavery that continues evolving into many hybrid forms. Slavery has not ended in the USA but has evolved. The road to freedom continues to be bleak and stony.

Stony the Road

James Weldon Johnson wrote the poem *Lift Every Voice and Sing,* set to music by his brother John Rosamond Johnson. On February 12. 1900, 500 children performed this song for the first time in honor of Lincoln's birthday. The National Association for the Advancement of Colored People (NAACP) adopted the poem as its official song. Today, *Lift Every Voice and Sing* has earned recognition as the Black National Anthem for its power in voicing the cry for liberation and affirmation for the African American people.

The poetic song is a prayer of thanksgiving and hope in God for God's faithfulness and freedom. The lyrics draw on the symbolic imagery in the liberation narrative of the biblical Exodus- God's dramatic, personal involvement in the rescue from slavery and as a helpful constant companion on the road to freedom in the "promised land." The lyrics narrate the history of slavery- the ongoing exploitation through the modern world's social, political, and economic structures. The anthem has broad appeal for all the discriminated poor of the world, the vast majority of exploited Black and Brown peoples. In the hymn, God is the loving cosmic God of justice who favors the world's poor, oppressed, weak, and miserable.

The poem traces African Americans' painful history beginning in the early 17th Century, their sale to white slavers who sold them in markets in the global colonies. One relives the violence, the anger, the disappointment, the betrayal, the capture, the bondage, the torture, and the long, arduous journey of forced immigration.

The poem does not delve deeply into the emotional trauma of separation from the God of the land and the closeness of God's love in the people. One can imagine the past vibrant life, the noisy laughter of children swimming naked in the fresh streams, running barefoot and carefree along well-trodden paths with the deer in the wild places, surrounded by the God of peace in all wild things. One can imagine the blissful companionship and fellowship of extended family in the village. One can imagine the warm protective presence of ancestral spirits in retelling the stories around the campfire. One can imagine the life-breath quickening the flesh bursting forth into high shrills and rhythmic dancing of women at the communal celebrations.

Lest we forget, one can imagine that day when the marauding gangs descended like the wolf upon the fold, scattering the sheep in all directions, causing chaos and unrest. Children, eyes agog, confused, bodies frozen, mouths wide open, the scene of turmoil unfolding. The children's game cut short, their eyes confused, their mouths wide open, and their song abruptly halted; the joyful, rhythmic individual notes of their songs scared heavenwards like frightened birds. One can imagine the machetes slitting open the throats of those who resisted—their limp bodies dropping to the ground in pools of blood. One can remember the torturous journey, the tired, bent bodies chained together, doggedly making their way to the holding places. The never-ending dirt tracks always seemed so long, appearing at first to go nowhere. The painful journey was made worse by tightly wrapped cords around wrists, neck, and ankles, breaking the skin, cutting deep, and burning into the flesh almost to the bone. The relentless hot African sun brought naught for their comfort, pouring sweat and salt into the gaping wounds. The crack of the whip tore the flesh, opening streams of blood. One recalls vividly, like a painting at sunset, silhouetted black hands in the dead of night, setting fire to the dry thatched roofs, razing to the ground what one once called home. One can imagine hearing the loud cries and lament of the older women, like Rachel in the Bible, at Ramah weeping for her children, forever gone never to return and refusing to be comforted.

Then there came those piercing screams, people losing their minds, first in the holding places before the journey, the nervous uncertainty of waiting before the dark descent into the hell in the hold of the ship. Then, at night, from the vessel's belly, one heard the shouts and the cries of the unsafe women above- daughters, wives, sisters, relatives- turned into slaves of sex for the sailors. Those who speak of The Middle Passage refer to the ordeal from the Guinea coast in West Africa to North America, Europe, South America, and the Caribbean islands.

The most significant loss for Africans was the loss of communion with others. Among Africans, the individual and society are kept intact by the concept of *ubuntu,* meaning the individual only exists entirely because of others. When the community falls apart, the individual falls apart. For Africans, the individual psyche exists because of the integrity of the corporate body and soul. The dawn of Western Civilization on the African Continent tore apart the seams of the individual and corporate soul and destroyed the cultural foundation of *ubuntu.* In the passage to the new world, the captive also faces trauma from filthy conditions, dehydration, dysentery, starvation, and scurvy. This deprivation of the necessities of life led to high mortality rates. On average, the "Guinea" slave ships that sailed from the Guinea Coast of Africa, carrying hundreds of slaves chained tightly to plank beds, lost 15% and up to a third of the captives. Many slaves, overwhelmed by depression and distress, committed suicide by throwing themselves into the Atlantic Ocean, where they met their watery graves. They say that large groups of sharks followed the ships waiting for the corpses of the dead.

It is impossible to imagine the full extent of devastation in the depths of the souls of those betrayed by dark Judases of their kind for the fixed price of filthy pieces of silver. The success of the Colonialist Empire rested on the institutional bedrock of slavery. The Western Church aligned with the State in its global land grab, world domination, and exploitation. The slaves found themselves caught in the systemic and structural machines of cultural capitalism. The State provided the politics, and religion supplied the Biblical theological rationale for capitalist, racist slavery.

Capitalism sustained by slave labor, or cheap labor, in any age, has no respect for life, self, the Lord God of this Universe, God's kingdom in this world, God's law of love understood as justice and respect for all God's children, other creatures, and the natural world. The evil institution of slavery, coupled with the corrupt institution of colonialism, injected the poison of individualism and capitalism into Africa. Individualistic religion and competitive capitalism's lifestyle continue to have a devastating effect on people's lives globally. Jesus preached a radically different lifestyle, the concept of the Kingdom of God, a non-competitive, cooperative organic community knit together in God and God's unconditional love. In this community, people live in *ubuntu*, acknowledging oneness with God and neighbor. The kingdom is that state achieved by the loss of Ego's fear, the place where there is no individualistic, competitive spirit, and everyone looks to the other's benefit. Jesus modeled this community while he was with his disciples. He lived off the grid, far away from the influence of the Ego's selfish world. Jesus connected with the world only when necessary, rendering to Caesar the things that are Caesar's and to God the things that are God's. His lifestyle manifested presence in this world, but not of the world, renouncing the egoist world, the flesh, and the devil.

James Weldon Johnson's poem, *Lift Every Voice and Sing*, now a religious hymn, describes Africans' journey and life to their eventual demise as slaves in America as "stony the road." Not much has significantly changed since the global African *Diaspora* since the early 15th Century. The road remains the "stony road" for all, except a few super-rich descendants of slaves in the USA. The present rise of religious nationalism aims to hold fast the Constitutional beliefs of one free white nation in America. Today, it is still ambiguous whether the American constitution is wide enough to include the descendants of slaves as equals in the United States. The Dred Scott decision ruled that African Americans were slaves, beasts of burden, and could not be afforded rights as humans and citizens. This decision still carries weight in the application of the Law when dealing with Blacks in the USA. Slavery has not ended but has evolved. Racism is the norm in American society. The establishment's intention to treat African Americans as chattel persists in policies such as Stand your Ground, the War on Drugs, Cradle to Prison, Police Brutality, and Stand and Frisk. These policies have a history that goes back to slavery, discriminating against African Americans because of their race. Many Blacks die while being arrested by white police officers who shoot to kill or choke to death. The last choking words of victims- I *cannot breathe*- speak volumes of the daily experience of Black lives in the USA. Young Black Americans fear the loss of life by just being outside their homes. Modern and Post-Modern Western civilization provides no guarantee for the survival of Blacks in the USA.

Western society's pillars, resting heavily upon patriarchal, racist, egoist, narcissist systems and structures of greed and exploitation, do not favor people of color in the USA. In Corporate America, there exists in the establishment, a glass ceiling for most Blacks and Browns. Only a few people of color managed to break through the racist economic barrier. The Corporate Ego allows for the idea of liberalism, small favors to Blacks, to create the illusion of a general systemic fair and equitable society. Those in power blame Blacks for their failure- for not trying hard enough. The distribution of wealth in the West exacerbates the plight of the Black poor. Most people in The Information Age know that 1% of the population control 99% of the wealth in capitalist democratic countries. In pandemics of war, pestilence, and disease, most Blacks and Browns, who live in poor city neighborhoods, are hit the hardest and suffer the most. Capitalist democracy turns people of color into a labor force mimicking slavery.

Lift Every Voice and Sing raises the issue of hope in times of suffering and distress. James Weldon Johnson is too intelligent to settle for false romantic faith- the spawned misguided belief that God without human partnership will magically redeem any bad situation. Others intelligibly talk of "realized hope" that includes the struggle for liberation and the end of corrupt structures and systems. All systems and networks of governance for order in Ego's world are flawed, no matter how good they work against others. Egoist systems and structures are respected by institutions and those who depend on them for survival. Jesus lived his life on society's fringes and proposed an alternative that focused on the least of people. Millennials, concerned about their future, recognize Ego's institutional corruption feel betrayed by the elderly leadership. Middle-class Blacks suffer from amnesia and anesthesia, are oblivious to poverty, and its natural causes in developed countries.

Several Black intellectuals have determined that liberalism does not help the cause of the poor and oppressed. For them, liberalism, the inadequate response to the poor with weak programs and projects, robs victims of their dignity by not allowing participation in shaping their destinies. Super-rich individuals create the illusion of assistance by donating large sums of aid to philanthropic projects. These charitable programs do not help because they aim to dismantle systems and structures of greed and exploitation. This point is driven home in Anand Giridharadas in his book, <u>Winners Take All,</u> *subtitled,* <u>The Elite Charade of Changing the World</u>. In the book, Giridharadas shows that global capitalism winners seek to help the losers without disturbing the market-friendly arrangements to keep winners at the top. Humanitarian aid is disingenuous and does not focus on the real needs of those who are poor.

American society has not changed much since Martin Luther King delivered his dream speech in 1963. The primary problem is racism-Whites thrive. At the same time, people of color are marginalized and poor. Institutional discriminatory policies deeply embedded in social, political, and economic structures are still based on race and class. The elderly and middle-class seek cheap peace, and the youths anxious about their future cry out for revolutionary change. The bourgeoisie religious still believes that politics should be separate and hope that the wicked will get their just reward one day. Weldon's poem is a prayer to the God of love hoping for equitable justice and fairness. This prayer is a rallying call to keep on the path of struggle, not forgetting the past life of giddy freedom with God in the land of birth.

Martin Luther King's strategy of *Satyagraha,* change by non-violence, must be reevaluated in the context of extreme violent poverty and racism. Many call for *responsible anarchy* as a strategy for change. Violence cannot be an option because God does not set aside the law prohibiting taking another's life. But God does allow for the deconstruction of the egoist, evil ideologies embedded in human systems and structures. God also topples Empires bent on exploitation, power, and control every five hundred years.

Jesus had no confidence in any egoist human model. He knew the priceless value of the house rule of non-tribal spirituality, the importance of love for cultural, social, political, economic, and personal transformation. Jesus proposed the Kingdom of God where individuals self-realized in God, mirrored God's unconditional love for others. Civilization's egoist thirst for self-service, self-preservation, power, control and greed hides God's light for this world, shields its eyes, and prefers the dark cave of paranoid ignorance and narcissism. This world is on a slippery slide to its destruction. Jesus proposed the new way for an abundant life based on God's unconditional love. Only God's love can undo the Ego's power over the human mind. Jesus proclaimed a message encouraging the Ego's loss, taking up the cross of love for God and others, and following as a disciple/ learner to mirror this love in this world.

An intelligent reading of the Christian scriptures through God's eyes of solidarity – the *"preferential option for the poor,"* or standing with the marginalized in society, helps in personal transformation, liberation, and empowerment for justice before peace in the world. God modeled solidarity in the act of creation, created all human beings with God's likeness and image, making humans a living soul wherein God as spirit dwells. John's gospel prologue confirms the oneness with God and oneness with others, declaring that God's Spirit the Christ lightens everyone coming into the world. The recognition that we are one with others and share God's same substance facilitates solidarity, empathy, and compassion in people's hearts for the powerless and voiceless. This kinship with others helps recognize systemic and structural oppression and effectively organize the struggle for justice before peace.

Astronauts encourage a trip into space to gain a Cosmic perspective of the world, a God's eye view of things as they are. In the letter to the

Ephesians, Paul encourages us to sit with the universal Christ in the heavenlies. From the aerial perspective, we see that God made us all one - sons and daughters of God- through Christ before creation 13.8 billion years ago. We see that there is only one world, one God, and one human race from cosmic space. There are no ideological, tribal, cultural, caste, religious, and geographic boundaries. Paul, in profound mystic prayer and life in God, found himself in the "image of God," wrote about "oneness" with others in Galatians:

> *There is neither Jew nor Gentile, slave or free, nor is there*
> *male or female. For you are all one in Christ.*

Only oneness or solidarity with God and those who suffer, those who live in the margins of society, will smoothen the stony road. Let us not stray from the places we met God. Let us not be drunk with the wine of this world. Let us not forget God, whose hand shadows us. Let us forever stand, faithful to God. Let us march on to victory.

THIRTEEN

Jesus died violently at the Roman government's hands at the request of the Temple Sanhedrin's religious authority. However, the scriptures say that he quietly went to death like a sheep to the slaughter, without a whimper. The Church, aligned with the State, dominated the view that Jesus led a non-violent life off the grid, preaching a message of non-violence. This sermon looks at violence in the modern world, identifies the primary sources of power, and grapples with violence as the means to the end.

Of Violence

My cousin, sentenced to house arrest because of COVID- 19, lives alone. She confesses that she has no love for books. Bored to death by solitary confinement, she decided to start reading the only book she found lying around- the dust-laden family Bible. She was disturbed and distressed by what she read. She had not gotten much beyond the Book of Genesis and decided to speak to me, who had Seminary training. She explained that she had to put the Bible down and had decided never to read anymore. When asked, she answered that the Bible was full of violence and murder. The violence that she could not escape in the news was also prevalent in the sacred scriptures- domestic violence, femicide, destruction of cities and nations. She was more alarmed that God also protected his persona and rights by using extreme force. The more she read convinced her that God was a God of violence. God also encouraged the people to pursue violent strategies to preserve God's honor, success, and prosperity.

The birth of a child is usually a joyous, peaceful event. The advent of Jesus was anything about the peace on earth that passes all understanding promised by the angels. His birth story included a violent egoist character prepared to practice infanticide to preserve his kingship and power. The birth story also records that violence occurred on a grand scale. The Cosmos was disturbed. Moons, stars, and planets were pulled together and tossed apart in space by immense gravitational force. Stars, Moons, and planets moved to align in the galaxy, accommodating the shift of Christ into this world and the man Jesus of Nazareth. Joseph's young family had to flee political violence in their native land and sought refuge in Egypt. When he and his family returned to their hometown to fill out the census, Joseph discovered the Empire had failed its promised housing program. The family had to look for whatever shelter was available. They found an annex, a lean-to usually reserved for the cover of animals during winter.

Jesus's life growing up was precarious and violent. Like all in Palestine, he endured the abuse of the Empire- state terrorism, violent repression, oppression, and exploitation. He spent his early life serving his father as a lowly carpenter in the family business. His peers likely joined the Zealot resistance to fight on the side of the poor, crying out for more. The elderly, like Zechariah and Simeon, raised hope, visions, and song. The young men would rise like the strong arm of God, striking with mighty power, overthrow monarchs and thrones, and deliver the people from the enemy. Mary, Jesus's mother, sang the Magnificat, praising God for forcefully changing the status of the rich by satisfying the hungry with good things and overthrowing kings and thrones. John Baptizing Jesus in the Jordan River John prophesied that Jesus's ministry would create a massive tectonic plate shift, causing a violent earthquake filling canyons and leveling the mountains. The Jubilee

Year promise, Jesus's message is a revolutionary protest action against the violence and death produced by capitalist greed.

Was Jesus consistently a man of non-violence? In the sermon from the famous hillside, Jesus encouraged a love for one's enemies, the practice of generosity, praying for those who treat you spitefully, turning the other cheek, and resistance to violence. Handling the text apart from the context is a pretext. Knowing the background, the people who Jesus was comforting will help avoid abuse of these texts. Also, context will avoid the temptation of generalizing that Jesus was not human, did not get angry, or used violence on occasion. Using a hermeneutic of suspicion and referencing other scriptural texts provides another perspective that adds to the whole picture concerning the man Jesus. In the Sermon on the Mount, who was Jesus's audience? Was he consoling a hurt people, consolidating a wounded nation, coordinating a movement first before opting for a particular strategy? Would Jesus give the same message if the oppressors were present?

Liberation Theologians speak from history's underside, the poor and voiceless context, pointing to the Temple incident to make a case for the use of violence. Jesus, in this incident, is portrayed as the angry zealot, violently throwing out greedy capitalists profiteering off the poor worshipers. Jesus took a rope, plaited it into a whip, upturned the tables, and drove out the money changers. A violent act in a place of worship!

Some say that Jesus was an extreme pacifist and use the following text to support their case: *Put up thy sword again into its place: for all, they that take up the sword shall perish with the sword.* This text, out of context, will always be a misapplication. Jesus, in context, is only talking to Peter, who he allowed to carry a sword. The State abuse this text to justify killing protesters who defend their rights with weapons. Those in power hypocritically dictate non-violence to the people while practicing violence on their subjects. Many are blind, limbless, and have even died in this world because of institutional violence.

Seasonal Empires preserve their reign successfully only by using violence for the sake of preservation of state law and order. A history survey reveals that reigning Empires destroy past ancient Empires, pounding them into the ground to build new ones on the old. In our era, we have witnessed the destruction of Mesopotamia and Babylon in Iraq's war on prime TV. Bombs have fallen, incinerated, and humiliated the ancient civilization of the Tigris and Euphrates. In the heat of the battle, adolescent American soldiers scrolled colorful messages in childish handwriting on missiles: *For Saddam, from the Fat Boy Posse."* According to the New York Times/ CBS, the survey found that 42% of the American public believed Saddam Hussein was directly responsible for the World Trade Center's September 11 attacks. An ABC News poll says that 55% thought Saddam Hussein supported Al-Qaeda financially and politically through his terror reign. We now know that the United States supported and financed *Al Qaeda*. President George Bush coldly issued clear instructions to his marines for the Iraqi people's liberation despite Iraqi bodies' cost. Maybe Bush meant the freedom of their souls. After using the good offices of UN sanctions and weapon inspections, Bush resorted to starvation tactics. Half a million children died when the infrastructure was severely damaged. After the invasion of Iraq, the US and its willing allies resorted to guile and opportunism. The US decided who would get the juicy "reconstruction" contracts. The UN Security Council voted unanimously to feed starving Iraqi people because of US-led sanctions and US-led war from the sale of Iraqi oil. The American people ended up paying for the war. At the same time, the oil companies, weapon manufacturers, arms dealers, and corporations involved in "reconstruction" worked to make direct gains. Many who benefited are old friends and former Bush/ Cheney/Rumsfeld/ Rice cabal employers. The "Tony/Bush" respective goverments assured the world that Operation Iraqi Freedom was about returning Iraqi oil to the Iraqi people via multinational companies like Shell, Chevron, and Haliburton. One may cynically ask whether these USA individuals and companies are closet Iraqi's?

The War Against Terror was not about terror. Also, the War on Iraq is not only about oil. The war is about the Empire's self-destructive impulse toward supremacy, domination, stranglehold, and global hegemony. The same motivation and process decimated the people of Argentina and Iraq- the weapons used against them differ- the IMF checkbook in Argentina and cruise missiles in Iraq.

Saddam Hussein was a despot, a menace to his people. But he did not possess weapons of mass destruction. If Saddam did possess nuclear weapons, Saddam would have used them against the USA and the "Bullied and Bought' ally invasion. Instead, Saddam received support from the US, remaining an ally until he decided to act unilaterally in the Persian Gulf. Saddam never supported Al-Qaeda. Disregarding what the propaganda machine says about dictators of the world, they are not the world's most significant threat. The greatest danger is what drives the political and economic engine and who pilots it. Noam Chomsky identifies the epicenter of the most considerable machine that is the danger to the world. In his writings on Indochina, Latin America, Iraq, Bosnia, the former Yugoslavia, Afghanistan, and the Middle East, Chomsky unmasks an ugly, manipulative, ruthless universe hidden underneath the layers of propaganda freedom. Yes, there is freedom or relative freedom in the epicenter of the Empire. What does this freedom mean in the dizzying maze of corridors that connect government, big business, and the business of managing public opinion?

Free speech, the *open market*, and the *free world* are anything but freedom. Among the many freedoms claimed in the US government, there is the freedom to murder, annihilate, and dominate others. There is the freedom to finance and sponsor despots across the world. There is also the freedom to arm, train, shelter terrorists, and overthrow and topple democratically elected governments. The freedom to stockpile and use weapons of mass destruction- chemical, biological, and nuclear, and the freedom to go to war with any country and government with which it disagrees. The Empire commits these in the name of liberty against humanity for the sake of "justice" and "righteousness." Attorney General John Ashcroft declared that US freedoms are "not *the grant of any government or document, but … our [The USA's] endowment from God.*" Armed with this mandate from heaven is the reason why the US refuses to judge itself by the same moral standards it judges others. The USA's good intentions in the world are to free native markets, to modernize its societies, liberate its women, and save their souls; this does not preclude murder and extermination of other people for their own good.

When President Bush announced strikes against Afghanistan, he said: "*This is the calling of the United States of America, the freest nation in the world, a nation built on fundamental values, that rejects hate, rejects violence, rejects murderers, rejects evil. And we will not tire*". No one knows the horrible foundation, the massacre of millions of indigenous people, the stealing of their lands, and the kidnapping and enslavement of millions of Black people from Africa to work the soil. Genocide and slavery provide the nation's economic and social underpinning. Chomsky also cites the genocide of Native- Americans. He once visited a graveyard and read the following words on a gravestone: *"Here lies an Indian woman, a Wampanoag, whose family and tribe gave of themselves and their land that this great nation might be born and grow."* The native Americans did not give their lives for the noble purpose of Empire building. The natives suffered slaughter and decimation, and dispersal in one of the greatest genocides in history. The United States survived this terrible past and emerged smelling sweet. They did not own up, nor did they make reparations. They did not apologize to Black Americans or Native Americans. Nor did they change their ways. Instead, America succeeded by using Hollywood for good publicity and propaganda. At its core, the US still reveals the callous heart of the American war machine, wholly insulated from the realities of war.

The driving force of the war machine is corporate globalization, also known as Imperial Capitalism. Corporate globalization needs a press that pretends to be free and courts that pretend to dispense justice. Money, goods, patents, and services are globalized. People's movements are restricted, and human rights are violated. In international treaties, one cannot expect justice on racial discrimination, chemical, nuclear weapons, greenhouse gas emissions, or climate change. The Empire exists for the obscene accumulation of power by any means necessary. The elite journey towards an ideal destination near the top of the world. The colonial outposts around the world report starvation deaths. The gap between those who make the decisions and those who have to suffer them is widening. Frustration and national disillusionment have become the perfect breeding ground for fascism. The people's fight, the goal, the vision of another world must include eliminating that distance. Tunnel-visioned leadership cannot see the intrinsic relationship between Empire, Global corporatization, racism, violence, and poverty. In the epicenter of the Empire, Republicans and Democrats are unaware of the existence of the Empire. Propaganda parades Democracy as development and progress. Democratic progress in the colonies means loss of self-governance, social upheavals, and ecological devastation. In Latin America, the Middle East, Afghanistan, Pakistan, Kashmir, peace means war, a daily battle against hunger, thirst, and violation of dignity for many in the world. The basis of war is often the result of a flawed peace due to systemic flaws.

The Empire is a violent place, like the universe where more massive galaxies, the bullies on the block, cannibalize smaller ones. In the fusion process, corporate entities' gravity smashes national states together, causing intense violence spots. In this black hole, everything gravitates by violent force and fuses into a singular point. We hope there will not be a massive nuclear explosion and the end of the world and life as we know it.

How did Jesus respond to the widespread violence and poverty in his world? The scriptures, in part, portray a perspective that Jesus was a contemplative and one who practiced peaceful engagement with the world. Commentators on the Bible make a case for Jesus's spiritual practices of *Satyagraha-* love force, and *ahimsa-* passive resistance. Unfortunately, there is no record of ahimsa's actual instances as activist protest marches, ashrams, social food pantries, or soup kitchens. Jesus, however, did practice as a healer in a health program that required no deductible.

Jesus proposed the concept of the Kingdom of God. The kingdom was a lifestyle of *being in the world and not of the world.* Did this mean a spirituality of escapism, turning a blind eye to suffering and poverty? Jesus encouraged giving *to Caesar what was Caesar's and to God what was God's.* Or did this mean wisely managing the art of dual citizenship in this world and not of this world? Jesus did die on the cross, the State's capital punishment for acts of treason against the Empire. Scholars remain unclear whether Jesus was a pacificist or a freedom fighter. Jesus did propose violence on a personal level. He said: *And if your right eye offends you, pluck it out, and cast it from you; for it is profitable for you that one of your members should perish, and not throw your whole body into hell.*

How does one respond to the Empire's pandemic violence institutionalized in social, political, and economic systems and structures and glorified in Liberal Capitalism globally? An effective response to the Empire depends on acknowledging and identifying the existence of the Empire. All reactions for reclaiming power and reducing the distance between those who have to suffer must include careful social, political, and economic analysis. At the outposts of the Empire's colonies, resilient governments must resist corporate threats of disinvestment and stand up as sovereign nations for their dignity. At the local level, nation-states must band together against the common enemy of Corporations. China paves the way for modeling a system based on a market economy that builds wealth and equitable prosperity. At the outposts, bribery must disappear, and corrupt leaders must be held accountable. There are shining examples of hope in the world. In Peru, there have been successful uprisings against corporate globalization. Argentina is trying to refashion a country from the ashes of the International Monetary Fund's havoc. In India, the movement against corporate globalization is gathering momentum. It is well on the way to becoming a real political force against political, religious fascism.

The responsible strategy is to confront the Empire, its thirst for power, racism, exploitation, and oppressive violence. We must name it like Jesus did when he called Caesar that old fox, deny it of oxygen, shame it, lay siege to it, and mock it. Artists in *Black Lives Matter* use street art, musicians use music and literature. Never a night goes by when comedians do not use their talent to name, identify, mock, and expose the Empire's vanities or officials. We must muster our stubbornness, joy, brilliance, and relentless spirit to tell our different stories different from those of the brainwashed. The Empire will disappear if we choose not to buy its ideas, version of history, wars, weapons, and the notion of what will happen. In any real democracy, people are the custodians of power and the makers of history.

This universe's laws center on community- connection, attraction, and a cosmic binding mechanism called love, compassion, and kindness. Teilhard de Chardin observed that we are evolving to our better selves and something better. The path that awaits us is the glorious path of love, mutuality (*ubuntu*), and care of person and neighbor. The alternative to terrorism or violence is justice. Where there is no justice, there is no peace- only violence.

FOURTEEN

*We live in the Anthropocene era, the epoch of humans commencing
a significant impact on Earth's geology and ecosystems. Humans
have unleashed a devastating effect on human life on the planet.
Noam Chomsky observes that humans are bent on suicide and cites
two instances- the Second World War and capitalism. Capitalism's
flexible system produces a maximum profit for the rich and quick
or slow death for the modern slave, the ordinary worker.*

*This sermon essay centers on global plutonomy, its beginnings in
the USA, its operation and influence in the modern world.*

Having Great Possessions

The letter of James outlines the practice of authentic faith while simultaneously denouncing dead beliefs. James addresses the wealthy, whose selfish-interested capitalist schemes serve the elite and work against the landless poor proletariat precariat. He writes:

*Weep and wail over the miserable fate descending upon you.
Your riches have rotted; your fine clothes moths have eaten; your
silver and gold have rusted away. You have piled up wealth in an
age that is near its close. The wages you never paid to the men who
mowed your fields are loud against you, and the outcry of the reapers
has reached the ears of the Lord of Hosts. You have lived on earth*

in wanton fattening yourselves like cattle-and the day for slaughter has come. You have condemned the innocent and murdered him.

In the preface of her book, Vandana Shiva states that in 2010, 388 millionaires controlled as much wealth as the bottom half of humanity. The number decreased to 177 in 2011; to 159 in 2012, 92 in 2013; 80 in 2014; and 62 in 2016. It faded to a mere 8 in 2017. At this rate, only one person may be in charge in 2023.

James' judgmental words announce awful news for the wealthy and good news for the precariat whose employment and income are insecure in the era of liberal capitalism, the age of disease and death for most and the destruction of the natural world. Society's pictorial depiction of the societal class divide in the USA is a cupola, a small dome on top of an enormous dome. The wealthy one-third occupies the luxurious security and comfort of the cupola. Two-thirds of the population live precariously, entirely dependent on the outcome of the financial Corporations' unpredictable reckless investment schemes. The LLCs and incorporated financial institutions present balanced budgets focused on profit margins based on quarterly earnings without considering the people's welfare. *In the land of the wolf, the worker is the prey.* In the USA's Capitalist world, the worker class, the proletariat, is as dead as the Dodo. Thus, there is a binary societal division based on wealth in the USA- the wealthy aristocrat and the precariat.

The is no hope or optimism of things getting better. What happens in the USA is the norm for national states globally. Corporations in the USA, helped by the American government, regularize global economic policy. Noam Chomsky, political philosopher, linguist, and activist, says that the American dream of social mobility has collapsed based on hard work ethic. Today workers cannot progress on hard work alone. Unprecedented inequality abounds. The disparity stems from extreme wealth concentrated in a small sector of the population- just

1%. The 1/10th super wealthy are the results from political hard work denying social power and changing economic policy over thirty years. Government policy, modified against the will of the larger population, has harmed democracy. Because elections are expensive and bought, both parties, Republican and Democrat, are in the major corporations' pockets. The government designed policies to increase and keep the wealth and power in the hands of the super-rich minority. The USA foreign policy makes sure that other nations toe the line or face violent reprisal.

The wealth disparity, the power shift to the wealthy few, and the reduction of democracy began early in the American Republic's history. The privileged and powerful sectors have never liked democracy. Democracy puts the power in the people's hands and takes it away from the rich and powerful. Where there is wealth, there is power.

In the initial formal structure of the Senate, the Senate controlled the power. Until a century ago, the Senate, not an elected office, comprised persons chosen by the wealthy aristocracy. Madison believed that the Senate should be more responsible men who "had sympathy for property owners and their rights." For the health of democracy, these rights had to be protected. The House of Representatives, closer to the population, performed a weaker role. In the Constitutional Debates, Madison said that society's primary concern has to "protect the minority of the opulent against the majority." He feared that if the poor voted freely like in England, they would organize to take away the rich's property. If this happened, this would be equivalent to carrying out land reform. For these reasons, the constitution had to prevent democracy, that is, the "tyranny of democracy." Madison talked in a pre-capitalist society where he assumed that the wealthy would be enlightened aristocrats, harmless figures working and dedicating themselves to the welfare of all. Instead, the majority decided upon Madison's constitutional system. Jefferson held the opposite view that democrats, the majority, should make the decisions, not the aristocrats. This schism between the wealthy aristocrats and democrats runs through American history to the present day.

Madison's solution was to reduce democracy by organizing the system to consolidate democracy in the wealthy's hands and fragmenting the population in many ways. He proposed a welfare state to reduce poverty with feeding schemes, and so on. These conflicting aspirations of the concentration of wealth and liberal social response make up the country's foundation. Richard Wilson and others say that inequality has a corrosive, harmful effect on both the wealthy and poor- poor social relations, consciousness, human life, and so on. Aristotle was right when he said: *To deal with the paradox in a democracy is by reducing inequality, not democracy.*

The USA's history is a constant conflict between two tendencies. Democracy from the population- a constant pressure from below- the underside of history. The rich are desirous of a powerful oligarchy or plutocracy from above. The 1960s, called the "Time of Troubles," were examples of significant democratization. Those, usually passive and apathetic, organized and shouted out their demands on the streets around passionate concerns- minority rights, Women's rights, environment, opposition to aggression, and general concern for the people.

In response to the civilizing effects of the 1960s, a regressive reaction to stop the tide of democracy followed. In <u>Requiem for the American Dream</u>, Noam Chomsky skewers the fundamental tenets of neoliberalism by revealing ten principles of concentration of wealth. These simple principles concentrate wealth among the few, are at work in America today, and include reducing democracy, shaping ideology, redesigning the economy, shifting the blame and burden onto the poor and the middle-class, attacking solidarity (*ubuntu*) of the people, particular interest running the regulators of finance, engineering election results, using aggressive force and fear tactics to keep the people in line, manufacturing consent through public relations using propaganda, and marginalizing the population from power.

Since the 1970s, there has been a coordinated business effort to beat back the actions of the 1960s for equal rights. The *Powell Memorandum, sent* to the Chamber of Commerce, a prominent business lobby, warned that business lost control over society. Supreme Court Justice Powell supported this observation. The Commerce believed that Leftists like Herbert Marcuse, Ralph Nader, the media, and the universities took over everything. This body also felt strongly that economic power was the means of freedom of only those in power. In 1975, the Trilateral Commission comprised of Europe, Japan, North America was also concerned and appalled by the democratizing of the 60s. For them, democracy was the excess of democracy.

In the USA, the Carter administration comprised those almost wholly drawn from the Trilateral commission's ranks. Because "special interest groups" were organizing to enter the political arena, the Commission felt that this imposed too much pressure on the government. The masses, therefore, had to return to a state of passivity and depoliticization. They were also concerned about the youth who were at the forefront of what was happening. They blamed the freedom on the schools, the universities, and the churches, which they called institutions of "indoctrination of the young." More "moderation in democracy" was proposed. The Trilateral Commission offered measures for indoctrination through education and control of the press. Since the 1970s, college tuition has skyrocketed. Lender's structure student loans, not like business debts or personal loans, to favor lenders. Students cannot declare bankruptcy and stay trapped by the debt for the rest of their lives.

The educational curriculum emphasized learning mechanical skills, which undermines creativity in both teacher and child. Slogans, *"teaching to the test," "No Child Left Behind,"* and *"Race to the Top."* Serve to undermine creativity in the student. The rise of Charter Schools siphons money from public schools into private institutions. This disinvestment hurts the children and the public school system. Data show that children do not perform better in Charter schools. In impoverished areas, the "masters of society" have decided to administer drugs to school children, ignoring that the school system, not the children, needs modification. The Trilateral Commission's study never mentions "private business" as a particular interest group. By definition, private business, recognized as a national interest, can have lobbyists, buy campaigns, staff the executive, and make decisions. The rest of the special interests, according to the commission, must be subdued for the sake of "democracy."

The significant backlash to the roaring 60s was redesigning the USA's economy, which shaped the world economy. Since the 1970s, the "masters of the human race" - wealthy owners of corporations- launched a concerted effort to shift the economy, increasing the role of financial institutions- banks, investment firms, insurance companies, and so on. Before this shift, in the 1950s, Financial institutions were a relatively small part of the economy. Their job entailed the distribution of unused assets like bank savings to productivity. A regulatory system until the late 1970s was in place to regulate banks. After World War II, the two victors - the United States and Britain- established the Bretton Woods international system, which handled capital based on the dollar linked to gold. In the 1950s and 60s, The International Monetary Fund (IMF) permitted supporting local government controls on capital export. The World Bank-supported state-run development projects. By the 1970s, regulatory rules on currencies were dismantled. This shift led to speculation on the money on an enormous scale.

As the rate of industrial production declined, there occurred a considerable flow of speculative capital. Traditional banks changed to risky investments, complex financial instruments, money manipulations, etc. The country shifted away from production. After the 50s and 60s, Boards of directors in major American corporations moved from industrial management and concern for their workers. Banks fill vacancies in board positions with business school persons skilled with financial trickery. Production companies could make more profit by playing the stock market than by producing in the USA. General Electric is a financial institution today, moving money around in complicated ways. This phenomenon is known as "financialization," the increased finance role in the economy, a corresponding decline in domestic production, and offshoring, which hollows the country's productive capacity for cheap labor elsewhere. Offshoring is profitable for multinational corporations- their managers, executives, shareholders- but harmful to the population. The places of production, where there are no health and safety standards, no environmental and safety standards - are places where people work in deplorable impoverished conditions. Apple produces in Taiwan -owned torture chambers in China. The profits make their way to the USA, to a class of millionaires and billionaires. There is also developing in China and Japan, and so on, an extremely wealthy class. China is an excellent example of the success of communism with a capitalist economy- only because of a strong State.

The "free trade" system in practice is not *free trade* at all. The free trade system puts working people in competition worldwide. The American worker competes with the worker in China. The USA exports operative values- concentration of wealth, tax on working people, deprivation of rights, exploitation, etc. This export of American values is an automatic consequence of designing trade systems to protect the wealthy and privileged.

In the manufacturing center in the United States, unemployment has recently reached the level of the Great Depression. There is a fundamental difference between the Great Depression and the present decline in jobs that will not come back unless there is a policy change. The "masters of society" have no interest in having large-scale manufacturing and jobs return to America's shores. The exploitation of super-cheap labor with no environmental constraints elsewhere yields high profits. Capital is free to move, but workers aren't free to move. Adam Smith pointed out that "*free circulation of labor*" is the foundation of any free trade system, but workers are pretty much stuck. Only the wealthy and the privileged are protected."

Lawmakers craft laws to increase worker insecurity. Alan Greenspan testified to Congress that running the economy is based on *"greater worker insecurity."* Insecure workers will not ask for decent wages, decent working conditions, benefits, or free association opportunities to unionize. Workers have maintained their lifestyles by working more hours and borrowing at inflated costs for the last thirty years. People go deeper into debt to survive, parading the illusion of wealth by buying worthless assets for consumption and a nest egg for the children's future education, etc.

People working longer hours mean no time and freedom for leisure, recreation, and reflection. With adults working, family systems collapse because there are no public services as in other comparable countries. If the situation persists, grandchildren will be managers and executives, sending jobs to Mexico or China. At the same time, the rest of the population does essential service at McDonald's. As a result, the people suffer while the masters of humankind live in luxury, making profits.

Financialization and offshoring lead to a vicious cycle of concentration of wealth and power among the select few. Producers make plenty of money elsewhere, which rationalizes shifting the burden of sustaining society onto the rest of the population. As a result, there have been attempts at regulating the business world. Still, these efforts have not been successful because of powerful lobbying from the business sector. Only the people can apply pressure by a counterforce to bring changes to the financial system's institutions.

Globally, a new category of people has evolved called the "plutonomy,"- those who have substantial wealth through the practice of "gush up" economics. They are the new consumers, the drivers of the economy. They came into being since the 70s when Reagan and Thatcher introduced significant financialization changes- speculation, complex financial statements, money manipulations, etc. To policymakers, the long-term future of the country does not matter. To those sectors of the population that sustain the full privilege, only corporate quarterly profits matter. The powerful State subsidizes research and development, provides a cushion, and provides bail-outs in times of trouble. The powerful military force globally maintains control of the world's financial interests and expansion, while three-quarters of the population decline into stagnation. Also, what happens to the next generation is even less of a concern. The plutonomy follows Adam Smith's maxim: *All for ourselves, nothing for anyone else.* More and more, the term *precariat*- the precarious proletariat, the working masses relegated to a precarious existence- is coming into use. The focus on bailing out and investing in the rich is heading toward a cliff. But, according to Citigroup, this is of no concern. The focus is only on profit for tomorrow, *"and who cares if our grandchildren won't have a world to live in."* In the USA, necro-capitalism has morphed into *nanny* capitalism that takes care of troubled corporate banks during financial crashes.

Plutonomy drives a deep wedge between the government-backed rich and the precarious poor. In China, the oppressed labor, controlled by the super-wealthy, is denied independent unions. Tens of thousands of protests occur annually. In India, the situation is more extreme. In some developing countries like Brazil, significant attempts are changing the harsh conditions of poverty and starvation. Citigroup analysis is still relevant- *the very rich plutonomy thrives, and the rest get by somehow.*

In the 50s and 60s, and earlier, the burden of taxes was on the wealthy. The tax system is now modified. The responsibility has shifted from the rich to the general populace, the precariat. The pretext is that the modification increases investments and jobs for the poor. Investments through the financial system, the stock market merely increase the profits of the plutonomy. Investments provide menial jobs for the precarious global proletariat. The truth is that only sustained giving money to the poor and working people who spend it on the economy stimulates production, acquisitions, increased job growth, etc. Even the COVID-19 government stimulus checks do not help the precariat, and government bail-outs only enrich the wealthy during crises. The Goldman Sachs group does not define investments as creating jobs for the welfare of those destined to lead precarious lives. Wealthy corporations such as General Electric pays zero taxes on their enormous profits. The burden of sustaining society has shifted onto the population living precariously.

The Democrats are moderate Republicans- Nelson Rockefeller Republicans. They view Bernie Sander's movement for precariat democracy as "Socialist." Bernie Sander's "political revolution" would not have surprised Dwight Eisenhower. The Republican Party has dedicated itself to racist global Capitalism, the welfare of the super-wealthy, and the corporate sector. They have turned away from protecting existing social assistance programs like social security, public education, health care, etc. To get votes, they mobilize evangelicals, racists, nativists, and globalization victims putting workers worldwide in competition with one another while protecting the privileged rich.

Plutonomy's tentacles and values have spread worldwide; its poison has contaminated much of the world. The full extent of the reality of this messed-up world has not yet dawned upon the wealthy. The wealthy construct high walls to hide behind, creating a sense of false security in a world falling apart. Dark expensive shades like a cloud have blinded the eyes of the rich. They cannot see that their clothes are moth-eaten, their silver and gold have rusted, the world is a mess, and the Imperial era is drawing to an end. The blind wealthy continue to rearrange deck chairs on a sinking ship called Liberal Capitalism, doing business as usual, robbing the poor worker in the marketplace.

But the judgmental prophetic word of God endures forever:

> *Weep and wail over the miserable fate descending upon you. Your riches have rotted; your fine clothes moths have eaten; your silver and gold have rusted away. You have piled up wealth in an age that is near its close. The wages you never paid to the men who mowed your fields are loud against you, and the outcry of the reapers has reached the ears of the Lord of Hosts. You have lived on earth in wanton fattening yourselves like cattle-and the day for slaughter has come. You have condemned the innocent and murdered him.*

There is an inextricable link between prosperity, consumerism, injustice, and oppression. The connection has catastrophic results for all God's people and the planet. In our insatiable appetites, we consume the world by living beyond our means on all levels- the use of banking cards, loans, and abuse of the planet's resources. Money becomes evil when not balanced by the prime responsibility of love of neighbor.

The obvious answers to the human dilemma must include kenosis and curbing our appetites by reducing lavish lifestyles. Kenosis is not merely denial or self-emptying. Kenosis creates space for God to fill one's total being with love for others. The Quakers have taught humankind the remarkable noteworthy tradition of simplicity, solidarity, and service.

FIFTEEN

History books are the work of intelligent evil or good humans.
James Baldwin correctly observed that all humans have the
propensity for good and evil. The shadows accompany the good.
The present era of Imperial predatory capitalism has birthed
a global catastrophe of pandemic proportions. T.S. Elliot
describes humans as hollow, "living and partly living." Only
human awakening and becoming can redeem hopelessness.

Study to be above reproach I Timothy 3:2

Those who are *"awoke"* scholars raise essential questions facing catastrophe in the modern era of the Empire's fall and decline. Those who have an awakened consciousness hear, feel, see, smell, and taste differently. Intuitively, they discern that powerful controlling magicians, false spirituality, loss of consciousness, and solidarity, have contributed considerably to society's pandemic dysfunction and corruption. Slavoj Zizek's objective, insightful, hopeful observation from the global crisis is that *"everything under heaven is chaotic and the situation excellent for new possibilities."*

Both Zizek and Cornel West agree that this is the time for raising consciousness through profound learning and robust philosophical engagement. The collapse crisis presents a deep sense of existential and social hopelessness. Evil, suffering, and death raise questions that demand human response for the sake of inner solace, solidarity, wellness, and social action for the sake of peace. The kairos moment, the apocalypse, serves to awaken the soul and kindles hope. Hope energizes the spirit for existential transformation and compassionate action in the world. The crisis functions as a mixed blessing of death and resurrection. The awakened mind thirsts after knowledge, the heart bleeds with compassion, and the integrated body longs to die so that others may live. Lenin said: *Learn, Learn, Learn.* Philosophy must again hit the fashion runway proudly and strut like a peacock, asking crucial questions.

The impact of the massive comet or asteroid 6-9 miles wide, 66 million years ago, devastated the global environment. A wide range of species was destroyed, including the dinosaurs. This destruction provided many evolutionary opportunities for new species. Mammals diversified, evolving into new forms such as horses, whales, bats, and primates. Human ancestors have been around about 6 million years, and modern humans evolved about 200,000 years ago. Civilization only began about 6,000 years ago, and industrialization only started in the early 19th Century.

Humans, a higher form of intelligence, have used intelligence to create a perfect storm of suicide-self destruction. The second world war ended the nuclear age, but humans have since devised new means to destroy everything. The end of the second world war began a new Anthropocene epoch- the current era in which human activity is the dominant influence on society, climate, and the environment.

Noam Chomsky says that in the 1970s, human intelligence moved on to its next step to destruction while protecting oneself through regimented capitalism. Intelligent humans have shifted capitalism into the neo-liberal era, eliminating their only means of protection. Decision-making moved from public institutions to private financial institutions immune from control and regulation. In the USA, private corporations use lobbyists to pay off the government and buy elections. Cornel West opines that American democracy is a failed experiment. Other parts of the world mimic this failed experiment in the West. Only China has used Capitalism for building wealth to serve all its people. The National States in the Empire, dependent on foreign assistance and investment, participate in their suicide, destruction of democracy, and the environment.

In the Anthropocene era, the "freedom of market "means servitude to unaccountable private institutions. Margaret Thatcher said: *"There is no society, just individuals."* Karl Marx observed that French repression was turning society into "a sack of potatoes. This amorphous group cannot work together." Financial Corporations seek to eliminate society's institutions that solidify and strengthen the community. Corporations dedicate themselves to profit and power maximation and the undermining of democracy. Corporate's neo-liberal policies create fear, anger, discontent, contempt, and hatred, contribute to the institutions' collapse, encouraging passivity among the majority. In the USA, real wages have disappeared since the 1970s and have since declined and stagnated. The rest of the world has followed suit. We now have a perfect global storm of social unrest developing.

The corporate-owned media deliberately and visually slows things down by using advertisements and contributes to ignorance, narrow understandings, weak responses, and selective coverage. Funders have influenced the media since the 19th Century. There is no such thing as "fake news" - only distorted views of the world. The actual news should discuss and video reality, showing the social, political, and economic situation. Since the 19th Century, media has depended on capital. It began in England when media succumbed to money-concentrated media advertising. The market plays a significant role in informing people about making choices. The media creating "informed customers" means customers who make irrational decisions. Today, a car advert sells sexism, masochism, and alternate reality and tells one nothing about the product's specifications- such as the car's engine capacity, durability, comfort, etc. The media drives consumerism by its social, political, and economic ideology.

We live in an age of profound awakening. We live in an age of dark ignorance. Michael Brooks, author, philosopher, talk-show host, activist, left a legacy of recorded media and literature warning of the Intellectual Dark Web (IDW), a maverick male intellectual group. The IDW believes that there are fundamental differences between men and women. Free speech is under siege, and identity politics is a toxic ideology tearing society apart. The IDW adds weight to the right-wing conservative narrative in the USA and other parts of the world, especially western Europe. In this dark environment where review happens, history does not inform consciousness, and hysterical passion drives the perverted anti-left plan for the social, political, and economic arena. In this fantastic alternative universe, facts, science, and history matters least or have no consequence.

Michael Brooks has influenced philosophers and reputed, world-renowned teachers like Slavoj Zizek and Cornel West. Brooks draws considerably from his Buddhist spiritual experience, sense and sensibility, and its detachment and awareness for mindfulness practices. He critiques those on the extreme left, the "super-woke" liberal material activists who despise ideological culture and concrete identity. For Brooks, culture does matter. But, like the famous scientist Neils Bohr who hung a horseshoe on top of his door for protection, Brooks also believes that ideology informs and energizes the physical body for action in reality. For Bohr and Brooks, there is material power in ideological myth and symbols. The proof was in people's lives- the evidence manifests in personal behavior and action towards others. For Brooks, supernatural beliefs go hand-in-hand with social activity. Predatory capitalism goes hand-in-hand with the existential. Feminism or womanism, or gender, goes hand-in-hand with global political, social, and economic issues. Brooks' pedagogy avoids dualism- the universal is related to the particular and the abstract to the concrete—all is held together to practice truth and truth-telling.

Brooks' teachings have a tremendous influence on Slavoj Zizek. Zizek notices that in the counter slogan used against All Lives Matter (ALM), white supremacists used abstract reason to counter the Black Lives Matter (BLM) slogan. White Supremacists in the USA, and other parts of the world, imposed the abstract argument to dominate the concrete context of racism in the USA. Zizek also points out typical examples of the use of the conceptual view from history. In Hitler's Germany, it was not correct to mention racism without mentioning anti-Semitism. It was also not fair to talk of Israel and not note Israel's racial attitude toward Palestine. Michael Brooks sees this retreat to the abstract as a liberal strategy of diversion and distraction to preserve the status quo. However, Zizek does point out exceptions. In the Hegelian paradox, Black Lives Matter (BLM) is a universal claim, and ALM particular. Stalin or Trump would argue that all lives *do not* matter. The modern era's poison is multiculturism, which performs as the abstract universal dominating the particular to keep the status quo and avoid blame.

West warns that in the "particular "or "concrete" discourse on class identity that "the end of the struggle must not only be about class identity. The discourse should include intellectual integrity, science, and solidarity. Class identity struggle- a fundamental lens- is permissible when used to view the world as we encounter the other identities in the global crisis. Suppose that it is only about identity one is concerned. He makes the case that somebody will mobilize the huge liberation struggle merely into a "class politic." Here, West references Adolf Reed Jnr, Fred Jameson, Slavoj Zizek, and Michael Brooks, who critique failed philosophical texts using particular, concrete contexts. Zizek argues that the battle of individual identity hysteria can remove hope from the more significant war of social unrest. Sun Tzu's advice in The Art of War was always to capture the higher ground in the war situation. Short-sighted corporals in the war against capitalism only see identity as the only problem, unable to see the relationship and connection in the big picture.

Brooks, West, and Zizek talk about the *ethical miracle* and the importance of culture in the context of hopelessness. Cultural ideology shapes humans and their social behavior. Religion- that is, good religion and its institutions- is crucial for a moral and ethical society. James Baldwin observed that there are goodness and evil in all people. All good people shadow callousness. Cornel West points to the importance of truth, morality, and ethics when there is no hope: "Moral-ethical integrity is truth-telling. The condition of telling the truth is to allow suffering to speak. If the kingdom of God is within you, everywhere you go, leave a little heaven behind." Meister Eckhart teaches the need for Christ, the epitome of incarnated morality in hell: "I would rather be with Christ in Hell than without Christ in Heaven." For Zizek, the moral-ethical miracle in the modern era is the courage of hopelessness. Liberalism, the mock appearance of goodness, denies creating and sustaining evil and even passes the buck onto others. In the present apocalypse, the nation must be global in its endeavors and intentional about being in the world and not of the world.

Goodness for Brooks, Zizek, and West is everywhere, like rain that falls without respect for person, persona, or identity. Dualism creates dichotomy, division, and distinction. Zizek points out that the Black revolution appropriated white thinkers' white dualist legacy and was more faithful to white thinkers' white heritage of separation. Zizek, the Hegelian-Marxist, quickly points to the paradox in the Haitian Revolution. In this revolution, they did not strictly follow the outcome of the French Revolution. Article 4 of the Haitian Constitution defines

Black, regardless of skin tone. In Mandela's South Africa, the oppressed included the oppressor in redeveloping the new South Africa.

Cornel West agrees that value and goodness are in all people, irrespective of culture and color. Blacks prized excellence and virtuosity in Western European culture. He says: "Blues musicians, deeply rooted in their individual and specific traditions, respected the excellence and virtuosity. Jazz musicians could not resist the classics. But while they listened, at the same time, they wrestled with death, dread, and domination for the sake of being human in the short trek on the road between the mother's womb to the tomb." Leo Tolstoy had a picture of Charles Dickens on his wall. Indian authors, despite criticism from patriots, revered Jane Austen and Charles Dickens. One Indian author even said he owed much to "Indian" authors named Charles Dickens and Jane Austen. Hopelessness is a global human struggle, not the private possession of any particular individual or ethnic group.

Michael Brooks, Slavoj Zizek, and Cornel West see the defeat of liberalism as essential in the context of predatory, necro- capitalism. For the world's future, the collapse of Trump's neo-fascism is imperative for Capitalism's destruction, as well as Joe Biden's and Kamala Harris's neo-liberalism. Biden's run for Presidency was a blow to the stomach of the left-wing tired- milk toast- liberalism that gave birth to Trump. Obama's phone call to support Biden over Trump was reckless. It ended Bernie Saunders' progressive march forward to democratic socialism for the impoverished White and Black precariat. Cornel West is more severe in his criticism of Obama's support of Biden. He sees Obama's Biden support as support for liberal, racist, fascist, predatory capital Imperialism. It seems for the moment, America has stalled fascism, but the rock of liberalism remains solid. America's progress is not dependent on the center's shifting to the left. Its preservation depends on how much it is prepared to eradicate the foundation and mother of capitalism's social dysfunction.

Americans have not been honest about what produced Trump. Nor are Americans prepared to seriously interrogate Obama's role as the blackhead of the Empire- as the facilitator of Wall Street reconstruction, greed, intensification of inequality, and poverty. Be aware that Black Lives Matter started under a Black President and administration. West's critique concludes that black power under a neo-liberal order cannot protect the poor black and white working-class. After 3.5 years of Trump, 60% of white males voted for Trump, 56% white females, 35% Latinos, 32% Asians, 31% Jews, 28% Queers, and 15% to 18% Black males. Note that 40% of the total population remains outside of the political process. In the USA, the neo-fascist sensibility has soaked in. Those desirous of change must speak to and engage this culture and offer an alternative to the neo-liberal order. Obsessive focus on demonization and getting rid of Trump, and fixing what is wrong, will not bring the necessary moral change. Zizek rightly and insightfully points out four political parties in the USA- Republican Conservative, Populist Republicans, Liberal Democrats, and Democratic Socialists. Independents choose any one of these categories out of necessity and occasion.

Brooks, West, and Zizek's- respectable great international teachers- note that we live in the moment of the colossal failure of the intelligentsia. The philosopher's responsible task is to help people see the global perspective, emphasizing the accumulation of facts and teaching students to think and ask the right questions. The intelligentsia and their institutions have accommodated fascist neo-liberal smartness and smugness. This collapsing world needs teachers with profound revolutionary courage accompanied by comedic humor, believing that they still fit in and want to act as transgressors in some symbolic way. The academic must bring deep sensitivity and passion to the task and focus on the powerless and working people's suffering. The neoliberal university generates subjects and agents who cannot see or disclose what lies hidden in its institution, hierarchy, and disciplinary vision of knowledge.

The reality of life is a war, and catastrophe is not an aberration but the daily routine of life for the most. Things cannot change by the American romantic, fantastic Gatsbyan wishes that tomorrow things will be better. Karl Marx would have proposed the healing energizing Hegelian dialectic that things *can* be different by collective action. In the present, what is going on and possible comes via contemplating the Utopian idea of what might have happened if things were other. Beckett suggests a more emotional, passionate response to the task at hand- *with real tears flowing, the Kierkegaardian leap without the Christian overlay of pious hollow beliefs, an alternate universe, a better after-life, heavenly, pious moralism's, and meaningless rituals.*

Modern philosophers discern that predatory capitalism is changing tremendously. Capitalism's success is the work of solid, strong states. Again, in the rule, there is the paradox exception. Black Lives Matter started in a robust repressive state with 800 military units worldwide that dropped 25,000 bombs every year during Obama's tenure. They say it is easier to imagine the end of the world than to imagine the possibility of another world. Brazilians walk around with slogans on tee-shirts: *This world is ending. It is time to think and plan for a new world.* Those in power know that this world is collapsing. They secretly prepare for different catastrophic scenarios like living in a bubble in total isolation from the poor worker. Some contemplate emigration into space. The world coming to an end is the *angst,* the felt hopelessness, and only if confronted will bring the courage of hope. There are vanguard efforts of hope realized in the world. Bolivia has come up with strategies that do not ruin the economy. China has learned to combine capitalism with socialism. Cornel West encourages one to embrace hopelessness as a comma and not a period. This welcome embrace of misery is the apocalyptic imagination. For Christians, it is the Jesus gospel, the whole meaning of the cross.

In the poem *The Hollow Men,* T.S. Elliott portrays liberalism as the hollow man, vacuous, empty of soul. *The liberty for wolves means death for the lambs.* The alternative paradigm in a failing Empire that produces hopelessness is the man Jesus in the Temple who threw out the money changers who professed religion. The money changers represent Hollow religion and its institutions, Wall Street, the Pentagon, Congress, Hollywood, the media, Harvard, Yale, Oxford, World Bank, International Monetary Fund, Plutonomy, Oligarchs, Plutocrats, Predatory Capitalism, etc. This tragic moment of barbaric greed is our wake-up call to a vocation of witness and waiting for the *perhaps,* the possibility, praying that things will not end as tragic-comedy. Jesus died on the cross. We must act wisely as serpents, harmless as doves- collectively- in an organized, moral, spiritual fashion with intellectual integrity, walking circumspectly among institutional sacred and secular gangsters, thugs, and spiritual fascists.

The COVID-19 is nature's new, *perhaps,* for possibility. Covid-19 must not be treated merely as a medical problem requiring only a technological response. Covid-19 is a social catastrophe and, serendipitously, presents the opportunity to become human to complete the evolutionary process. The State's reaction to Covid-19 proves the efficacy of socialism. Beyond all imagination, States have responded in a leftist-socialist fashion that defies logic. Money has been pouring into healthcare, education, and local institutions for employment and aid. Stimulus sent directly to the precariat have brought much-needed temporary relief. It is high time for the hollow man to follow suit with a spirituality that defies callousness and mediocrity. Jesus, the man, caught smack in the middle of the collapse of the Roman Empire, responded from within life off the grid, with the message of unconditional love, stood with the poor, crying out for more. He left this legacy for all the precariat, the intelligentsia, the teachers, the wealthy, the institutional thugs and gangsters, etc. The debate lies in suspense as the new births. The future is what we make of today. Heaven remains perfect, and everything under heaven is chaotic, full of possibility. There are two types of religion. One waits for a distant God, and the other participates with the God engaged in the mission of radical love.

SIXTEEN

Most religious traditions look upon the world and the human body as evil. The philosophy of dualism separates God from creation and humans from the rest of the planet. Doctrines scale down God into human form. Beliefs elevate the Devil to a status a little less than God, significantly influencing humans and the world. Perceptions about God influence attitudes towards others and the planet. Can the confessional words for initiation- the world, flesh, and Devil, be understood in a way that influences positive relationships with self, others, and the world?

The World, the Flesh, and the Devil

The catholic tradition of initiation through baptism into the church requires all to renounce Satan and all the spiritual forces of wickedness that rebel against God, the evil powers of this world that corrupt and destroy God's creatures, and all sinful desires that draw one from the love of God. Unfortunately, these confessional words imprinted on the Christian psyche have contributed much to how humans view the world and others.

Philosophy borrowed from the Greeks has entrenched a negative, skeptical attitude and abuse of creation. Dualism, the dominant strand in Western philosophy, succeeded in imprinting the shared belief that everything is disconnected and unrelated in the psyche. Fed with mother's milk, humans learn to fear social distance, divide, and compete early in life. In an industrialized society, division, competition, and deprivation are the new normal. Because God practices apartheid from humans and the rest of creation, humans do the same. The way of the world, the separation method, has influenced the church's relationship with society. Most church folks believe strongly that the human body, the Devil, and his works in the world are evil. Religious people advise the separation of politics and religion. Politics, for some, is no less the work of the Devil. For Catholics, the sources of evil, the world, the flesh, and the Devil form a hierarchical model representing the spiral of violence. The world is at the bottom, the meat in the middle, and the Devil at the top. If evil and violence are unrecognized at the first level, corruption in the other stories is inevitable.

The world includes egoist civilization, how groups, cultures, institutions, and nations organize themselves for fleshly control. Evil is a past master at disguise, hides inside their systems and stuctural creations. Humans refuse to critique their majestic, proud products and fail to see the dark side. Not many are wont to bite the hand that feeds and culturally admire the vice. The Devil represents the personification of power, hard to recognize because of its mastery at disguise, is even idolized as reasonable and necessary. The Devil is sanctified, and legitimizes violence to control angry mobs out of control.

The philosophy of dualism deeply embeds the confessional of renouncing the world, flesh, and Devil, the model of sources of evil, and belief in the spiral of violence. When God created the universe by the Word, the extension of God's universal spirit, God knit together the elements uniting the matter. In Genesis, God combined with the dust, becoming one with humans. There was no separation between humans and God, who is spirit. God, vast and omnipresent, the plus and overplus in creation, fills every created thing. God saturates everything.

Over the millions of years of the brain's development, human consciousness created the illusion of separation between matter and

God's spirit. The illusion has direct consequences on human behavior, function in the social arena, and the planet. The illusion of duality impacts individual human life. It affects choices between inner goodness for others and disingenuous actions for selfish interest. The model of spiral levels of violence functions well with infantile faith and the illusion of dualist philosophy. Everything falls apart without binary philosophical thinking.

Can the universe function without dualism? Science proves that things function and relate with unity and oneness. The brain does a phenomenal job of helping the total body operate as a single unit. The central nervous system in vertebrates wonderfully and mysteriously connects and integrates the whole body, mind, and consciousness. The brain comprises three essential parts- the seat of emotions, the center of thought, and the motor center. The cerebrum and hippocampus work together to position limbs. The cerebrum, the most prominent part of the brain structure, and the forebrain is the seat of consciousness. The cerebrum's outer portion, the cerebral cortex, processes sensory and motor information and enables consciousness, the ability to consider ourselves and the outside world. In the brain, emotions, motor sensors, and consciousness work holistically together.

The Enneagram, a tool for self-discovery, proves that human behavior can be analyzed and understood as singular integrated persons. The Enneagram, a tool for self-awareness, helps understand human personality types for healthy relationships and meaningful and purposeful living. The human analysis tool understands that humans are far too complex to fit into simple separated categories. The human personality is a dynamic organism of a triad of gut (instinctive), heart (feeling), and head (thinking).

After thousands of years of dualist thinking in the West, humans have grown accustomed to acting and behaving in separating and categorizing ways. This apartheid thinking has contributed to competition, division, and violence. Our philosophical ancestors have deeded the concept of dualism that separates matter from energy, physics from metaphysics, and the sacred world from the secular world. This divisive philosophy encourages binary thinking and unhealthy erratic disingenuous behavior that appears selectively moral, partially moral, or outright immoral. Fundamentalist religious believers love those within the camp and discriminate against those who are different. Dualistic philosophy in the West remains the mental fodder for the racist apartheid and meanness that stokes racism, capitalist exploitation, misogyny, homophobia, and other symptoms of a dysfunctional society.

Western dualist theologians, disturbed and threatened by the magnitude of the East's pantheistic experience of God's saturation in creation, declared pantheism a heresy. These theologians, culturally challenged, semantically proposed panentheism as the mental solution to the "pagan" threat invading the West. In panentheism, the philosophy of dualism remains intact. God is thought of as present but remains still separated from evil creatures like those in other tribal religious cultures.

Traditional theology ignored the pantheism in the scriptures preserved in the New Testament Canon. Paul and his movement experienced God as the one in whom one lived and had being. Early mystics protested with their feet, walking away in disgust as the church morphed into institutionalized religion. The mystics walked away into the desert places, knowing God as not a separated recluse but a direct, unmediated experience. Dualist theologians saw immense value in building an institutional ziggurat to reach the distant God. Religion, like a ziggurat, connects the gap between a distant God and makes it possible for the believer to be close to God while practicing clerical mandated social distance. Mystics have always experienced God beyond a mental concept. God is a rupturing encounter for mystics, a direct experience within body, mind, and spirit. God for mystics is an intimate union of the essence, the likeness, and image of God.

Institutional religion's success in the world thrives on aligning sacred Biblical texts with dualistic, binary, or sectarian thinking. Dualist thinking separates God from creation, sustains tribal religion, divides nations, fragments societies, and proves lucrative. Christians worship God in a spirit of division. 11 o'clock on Sunday mornings is the most divided hour of global Christendom. Dualism and binary thinking philosophy rationalize fear and prejudice, stoking populist racism, sexism, homophobia, xenophobia, etc. Dualism thinking creates duplicitous behavior between Sunday worship and weekday service. Dualist thought affects the strength of community and action in the world. Most believers use the church for public convenience- only when necessary- like automobiles needing occasional fill-ups. Jesus was concerned about this mechanical, stop-and-start enspirited relationship with God. The early church in apocalyptic times preached against mediocrity, stating that God spews out those who are lukewarm.

Tradition's rationale and philosophy in the rite of baptism creates an illusion that scrubs away billions of years of unbroken, intimate connection and love relationship with God, God's creatures, and the Cosmos. God set into motion building a dwelling place in this planet 4,5 billion years ago. The first human species with a tiny brain appeared between 5 and 7 million years ago. Modern humans walked upright on the planet 300,000 years ago with a brain three times the size of the earliest ancestors. The developed 3.5 lb. brain developed strategies of survival based on individualistic competition, greed, hoarding, and thoughts of division and privation. The human brain created its grandest illusion: God as spirit, the universal Christ, vacated this evil world, dwells in heaven, and operates through human institutions and intermediaries. Gullible humans have forgotten that God is in magnitude beyond space, time, imagination, omnipresent, and saturates this world with the universal spirit. God is one and is as close to humans as the jugular vein. God also has a name that means "God with us."

As humans, we exist as specks in a Cosmos of infinite magnitude, united by the principle of unifying spirit. The idea of separation and philosophy of dualism is a young illusionary thought of a 2.5lb mass of jelly resulting from a filled brain cavity not too long ago. Scientists have discovered that the brain is shrinking, and humans have fully developed physically. However, humans have yet to evolve into the total human capacity, to live bathed in the universal cosmic energy, the only reality that lasts forever, namely unconditional love. Only egoistic human religion stands in the way of union with this love. Rabbi Herschel sees religious beliefs as impeding the flow of the goodness of love on this planet. He says:

> *"It is customary to blame secularism for the eclipse of religion in modern society. But it would be more honest to blame religion for its own beliefs. Religion declined not because people refuted religion but because it became irrelevant, dull, oppressive, and insipid. When faith becomes an heirloom rather than a living fountain, when religion speaks only on the name of authority rather than the voice of compassion- it becomes meaningless."*

The baptismal rite does not call neophytes to forsake the world, the flesh, and the Devil to enter a dull, oppressive, insipid institution. Instead, baptism reminds God's creation, uniting God and dust, original goodness, and love. Baptism *remembers* one into this life of union with the dynamic universal spirit. Baptism also teaches us about the lost way of tradition- its dualism, binary thinking, beliefs, and broken mediatory religion supplants God's close, garden walk with the Beloved. If there exists a model of the spiral of violence of the world, flesh, and Devil, God is in it, not distanced from it. God, through Baptism, calls us into the partnership of struggle to fight, not to flee, and be the yeast, leaven, and light.

SEVENTEEN

In an era of the Empire's collapse and social unrest, Jesus did not settle on any one particular populist cause. Instead, he proposed an umbrella solution for the widespread psychological hysteria and systemic social dysfunction caused by the Empire. He left this healing legacy for all times and seasons. His answer to the international human dilemma still divides believers and scoffers. What did Jesus propose? The answer lies embedded in the story of Nicodemus's private consultation with him. Jesus's universal response to Nicodemus is pertinent for the redemption of personal trauma and global apocalypse.

You must be Born Again

Most scholars concur that John's gospel was the last gospel to be written. It followed the Synoptic gospels of Mark, Matthew, and Luke. Among traditional scholars, there is consensus that Mark is the earliest gospel, followed by Matthew and then Luke. Context and message are the two main criteria for determining the relative order and ages of the gospels. Most scholars agree that Matthew's gospel preceded Luke because of its indisputable Jewish cultural context and message. The evidence supporting the latest placement of Luke is twofold- Luke concentrated on the gentile world, and the gospel spread from Jerusalem. Luke's gospel, written in two parts, also contains the biography of Paul, a latecomer in the Jesus movement, unknown to Jesus and the first disciples of "Jerusalem."

There is strong evidence to support John's gospel even preceding all the synoptic gospels. Scholars Robert Miller, Marcus Borg, John Dominic Crossan, and Stephen J. Patterson highlight the apocalyptic background to John's gospel. This observation is vital for the placing and importance of John's gospel. Widespread trauma in pandemic social, political, and economic unrest raises the level of personal hysteria and the need for saviors. In apocalyptic times, people retreat from pain centers worldwide, seeking answers from deep within the soul. Such times also raise profound questions about failed religion and its efficacy. Social and psychological scientists have observed that humans in deep crisis turn inwards to God for help and trustworthy teachers. Jesus arrived at the opportune time, enlightened, well-seasoned, and leavened to respond to those hurting and hoping.

The mediated conceptual God in religion managed by unspiritual corrupt political clerics had no tricks in the bag of faith to offer to heal the nation's stripes. On the contrary, the people longed for the close God, a direct encounter not found in institutional religion. Jesus, the wandering mystic prophet-teacher, his mendicant lifestyle, his healing message, and an incarnational theology of the God present in creation evoked a response of deep trust and confidence deep within the people's soul.

Jesus the mystic taught about *ab-original* goodness, or original conscience, resident deep within the true self, the soul. Jesus never convinced people by fear of punishment, guilt, and shame of original sin. Instead, Jesus positively moved his hearers. He reminded them that God created all humans with original goodness. Jesus was born into an indigenous culture that lived comfortably in God's intimate presence and companionship. The Greek philosophy of dualism, the idea that God dwelt separately from creation, was foreign to the psyche of Jesus. Jesus knew that God created all humans by combining borrowed dust with divine essence, God's spirit, the universal Christ, the anointed one.

Jesus was aware of Ego's mind imprisonment with the idea that God would never dwell intimately with humans. Therefore, Jesus did not start another religious device but offered simple advice for encountering and living in God by renewing the mind and losing Ego consciousness. Humans, to encounter God, had to leave Ego, the false self behind, and live in God as contemplatives in a liminal space called the kingdom of God or Heaven on earth.

The apocalypse, the in-between time before the new, is more about God's revelation of the new order than a world coming apart at the seams. John portrays Christ in Jesus as the revealed order, the message of truth for Ego's imaginary dream world. In times of crisis, mystics like Jesus, by word and deed, signal the crucial need for existential union with God for personal health, social welfare, and preservation of the planet. The mystical experience of oneness, or unitive consciousness, was essential in Jesus's way for truth and life. Jesus, hours before his murder, hoped and prayed that those he rescued from dead religion might receive the perfect gift, the gift of unity with God:

> *21That they all may be one; as thou, Father, art in me, and I in thee, that they also may be one in us: that the world may believe that thou hast sent me. 22And the glory which thou gavest me I have given them; that they may be one, even as we are one: 23I in them, and thou in me, that they may be made perfect in one; and that the world may know that thou hast sent me, and hast loved them, as thou hast loved me.*

The gift of oneness is unitive consciousness or divination. The source of life that flows from being in God is *ab-original* goodness. Luke explains this lifestyle as one living, moving, and having one's being in God. Jesus personally lived out this gift in his short history of incarnated life. His vocation was a teacher who stood squarely in the ancient universal indigenous spiritual wisdom tradition of oneness with God. He fervently prayed that his followers know his discovered secret of unitive consciousness or oneness with divinity. His *High Priestly Prayer* hoped that God would grant his learners a glimpse of God's inner glory already in their lives. This inner glory is always there and never leaves. God increases when Ego dissolves, and the illusory notion that God is not present dissipates.

He had this one-ness glory as an ordinary man but chose to empty it as a slave to others in his earthly ministry. The "oneness," "union," or unitive consciousness is more important and necessary than the ideology of solidarity, ubuntu, or community. Those who strive for justice without God's presence end up as corrupt officers for themselves. Without oneness with God, there can be no ubuntu or community or moral righteousness. Oneness is a personal lifestyle for the well-being of others. Jesus prayed that his disciples would live in God's presence-walk and talk with God in God's kingdom of Heaven on earth before death. Jesus prayed that they might be one in that incredibly intimate way he and God shared life.

The wisdom mystic tradition embraces the prophetic tradition. Prophets know unitive consciousness with God. True prophets only speak out of their life in God. Prophets sit on the margins of institutional religion and organizations. Like all prophets, Jesus prophesied against the fleshly compulsions and excesses of superficial, legalist, institutional religion that produces perversion and depression. He severely criticized clerics, their blatant religious bigotry, and their apathy towards those hurting and hoping. For this, Jesus was convicted and splayed on the cross to die as a common criminal. His disciples faced inevitable abandonment and uncertainty in troubling times after his departure. Jesus knew that only the mystic spirituality and lifestyle would suffice. He hoped that solidarity with God and others would be a constant refrain in his learners' prayers.

The wisdom tradition of unitive consciousness with God is not very apparent in the later gospels of Mark, Matthew, and Luke. Luke's narrative of the Day of Pentecost is an apology that explains particular human ecstatic worship practice. It cannot replace Jesus's mystic spirituality, the lifestyle of self-awareness, consciousness, and morality. Modern Christians mistake charismatic worship experience for the ancient mysterious wisdom tradition of Jesus. Among all the apostles, Paul was the only one who knew of the mystic tradition. The Jesus movement started in the ancient indigenous mystic tradition. Within four hundred years of church tradition, Jesus's gospel and spirituality dissipated into an outward form of religion that denied God's inner power. Religion is a system complete with a constitution, religious rituals, and beliefs offensive to true teachers and prophets.

The early mystics of the first 500 years of Christianity were greatly offended by the movement to institutionalize. They left to live with Christ in the desert spaces of the collapsing Roman Empire. Like Amos, prophets, and teachers, attentive to God's word, say that religion turns justice into bitterness and cast righteousness to the ground.

> *"I hate, I despise your religious festivals;*
> *Your assemblies are a stench to me.*
> *22Even though you bring me burnt offerings and grain offerings,*
> *I will not accept them.*
> *Though you bring choice fellowship offerings,*
> *I will have no regard for them.*
> *23Away with the noise of your songs!*
> *I will not listen to the music of your harps.*
> *24But let justice roll on like a river,*
> *Righteousness like a never-failing stream!*

Jesus's prayed that his disciples and their disciples embrace the mystic wisdom prophetic tradition. His rationale was that his learners would complete his mandated mission of establishing God's Kingdom's reign of righteousness in this world. The Kingdom of God Jesus spoke about was the space where one practiced contemplation for learning and practical wisdom for goodness to others. But, unfortunately, the institutional system deliberately suppressed knowledge, tradition, and the mystic gospel of Jesus preserved in John's gospel.

What is Jesus's gospel? Without understanding God's creation of humans, and the physical structure of the human body, it would be impossible to glean Jesus's simple gospel message for direct union with God. There is more clarity of the Jesus gospel in John's gospel. John's gospel of repentance from Sin, *not* sins, dealt with the only Sin of humans- separation from God. At the same time, the other gospels centered on human failures called sins and salvation through a human system where God is an idea living in an alternate universe. The synoptic gospels rationalize mediatory salvation by having a thick overlay of cultural control politics - Matthew over Jews, Luke over Gentiles, etc. For disingenuous reasons of politics and economy, authoritarian elitism keeps the organic Jesus gospel of grassroots empowerment a subdued secret.

Humans possess two physical bodies and a spirit body holding God's essential nature of unconditional love. Over millions of years, the physical body of the brain developed in size and self-consciousness of an imaginary state of being that can live separate and independent from the physical structure and God. This ego-consciousness, primarily a belief that evolved as a false self, empowers independent decisions and life choices. With the rise of Ego came the loss of *ab-original* conscience and existential unitive consciousness. Jesus's gospel strongly encouraged the loss of this false self and its selfish influence in decision and action. Jesus called his followers into contemplative student life living in oneness with God. In this prayerful living state, one constantly question, learns, loves others, and cares for God's heavenly home, the planet. The false self, an imaginary state of being, has succeeded in genetically implanting behavior consistent with separation from God. Based on Greek dualist philosophy, religion declares this divorced state and distant existence of God as sound doctrine. It cancels and stigmatizes those who seek union with God or acknowledge God within. Jesus's gospel encouraged seeking life in the kingdom, losing the self, knowing the God within, and following God's love for life at the crossroads. The church of God is not the kingdom of God. The church, at its best, seeks to become God's kingdom.

Nicodemus, who reached the highest level in his religion, heard of Jesus's good gospel of mystic spirit leading to truth, good works, good relationships, and profound spirituality. He realized that his faith crisis was due to a blind obsession with flawed religion aligned with the State in a rapidly changing world. The more he listened to the teaching of Jesus, Nicodemus embraced the wisdom that God can be a life experience regardless of culture and religion. Nicodemus saw Christ, God's glory in the man Jesus. He desired this glory, seeking Jesus in the dark of night. He knew that Jesus would lead him out of the darkness of flawed religion to light and salvation. Jesus compassionately responded to Nicodemus's strengths of humility, inquiring spirit, courage, and willingness to learn. He advised a radical spiritual makeover for Nicodemus. *You must be born again!* Tradition misunderstands these words of advice of rebirth to Nicodemus. Indeed, it was not reentry into the mother's womb. Nor was it church baptism or Spirit baptism. Jesus meant a mystic resurrection, the leading of God's spirit into God's bosom, full of truth, the womb of God.

The present apocalypse is evil manifested in principalities, powers, and thrones. These are premodern terms for corporations, institutions, nation-states, ideologies of supremacy, politics, economics, societies, and organizations that demand blind allegiance. In the USA, poverty, racism, and violence are uncontrollable. In India, thousands commit suicide because of debt to predatory lenders, the "free-market system" lie, and the inability to afford corporations' exorbitant prices for genetically modified seeds. In South Africa, new government officials cannot control their compulsive drive for looting the state treasury. The result is poor government delivery service and rampant poverty. Globally, poverty and hunger are the majority's constant shadows. At the same time, the middle-class and wealthy live in protected isolation and moderate to extreme luxury.

What does God reveal amidst the apocalypse of widespread destruction, corruption, social dysfunction, death, disease, poverty, pollution, and a rapidly changing world? God at one time sent the born-again word Jesus who marched to a different drumbeat to the established religion, preaching the way of direct encounter and union with the Christ in creation. In this present apocalypse of revelation, God sends a new kind of human, as the word. All, irrespective of religion, can be this word, heeding: *You must be born again. Leave Ego behind. Live into your divinity!*

EIGHTEEN

The modern era raises the need for qualified leadership in the local, national, and international church system. Jesus said that the children of today are much wiser than previous generations. Those who seek a deeper relationship with God in creation vote with their feet, leaving the institutional Church in droves. Covid 19 has pronounced a death blow to a dying church. What would it take for the Church to survive the apocalypse, this moment of revelation? The church system has missed its 100,000 km check-up. It now needs a complete overhaul.

Leadership for Effective Church Ministry in the Modern Era

Clergy education, pastoral competence, and spirituality are severe considerations for leadership positions in the Church today. The present generation is more intelligent, more academically educated, experienced, and talented than clergy who master them. The archaic patriarchal political structure based on the model of the English feudal system favors the ordained oligarchy. When elections encounter a stalemate in a decision, the Church's political structure relegates responsibility to its most senior ordained leaders. The institution does not live by the adage of *government strictly by the people for the people.* The Church considers itself "catholic," meaning that the clergy is *"mfundisi,"* the controlling expert in all life matters. The clergy's general demeaning attitude toward the laity is patriarchal and patronizing. The Master - Slave or Master-Servant Marxian analysis applies in global and local contexts even when the laity runs programs. Servant leadership, a hackneyed phrase, means clergy are the boss, and the people are the servants. The usual ubiquitous refrain of obedient laity is Father *knows best.*

Kester Brewin, the son of a clergyman, points out that the problem in the Church is its Evangelical fundamentalist theology, power politics, and authoritarian structures. This list should add discipleship or learning, response to social unrest, and practical spirituality for transportation or evolution into being a human. The present structures and systems of the Church are rigid, controlling, hierarchical, paranoid, and selfish. A master plan orders the system to keep people infantile, underdeveloped, or undeveloped. Positional power coupled with the master plan of the system serves the position and not the whole entity. Organic order, a radical concept for present leadership, is necessary for the organization that seeks not to violate its people. The archaic institutional system and authoritarian structure are not the only issues contributing to a leadership crisis in the Church. One cannot underestimate the importance of the gospel and life of Jesus living off the grid, practicing contemplative spirituality living in union with the universal Christ within creation and the inner self for sound leadership.

Discipleship or learning for a solid educational foundation is an essential component for informed decisive leadership. Rational and critical thinking is necessary for navigation in a rapidly changing and expanding world. In the present Information Age, instruction respecting the global context and global solidarity or ubuntu make for successful outcomes for a just and fair world. We now live on a planet reduced to the size of a global village. Therefore, the local Church's obsessive preoccupation must shift from its survival strategies of church growth and internal health. Instead, it must concentrate on becoming a missional church passionately concerned with social unrest, dysfunction, and corruption in the neighborhood and the world. The missional church differs from the mission church, whose main thrust is the ideological conversion of people into an alternate universe separated from this world.

The Church must invest in leaders in three main areas- education, training in pastoral ministry, and spirituality. Church practice since the late 60s has slipped away from the traditional trinitarian Anglican wisdom grounded in the integrated "study" of Scripture, Tradition, and Reason- the three-legged stool. In the late 60s, Charismatics added a fourth leg, namely, Subjective Experience. The fourth leg of "subjective experience" gradually gained importance and ascendency. Today "subjective experience" rules supreme in the majority of local charismatic congregations.

The charismatic renewal and the rise of Evangelical Fundamentalism dealt a severe blow to the ancient English wisdom tradition. Personal libraries shrunk to a few favorite singular verses of some of the 66 books of the Protestant Bible. The Holy Spirit now leads away from all the Truth in the modern world. American Evangelism in Southern Africa thrives operating from an alternate universe, believing alternate "facts," disbelief in Science, hatred of other cultures, and gut intuitive wisdom unsupported by logic and reason. Disciples/ Students refuse to acknowledge a changing world and rapidly expanding Cosmos. These learners dismiss valuable global insights from others in other parts of the world. Learning institutions center their studies narrowly on local contexts, deliberately disregarding information in similar contexts elsewhere. Accredited teachers focus on imparting knowledge rather than training their wards to think critically and act decisively with well-researched opinions.

Academic qualifications for clergy have been gradually declining in Southern Africa. Even before the 60s, the Church accepted candidates who did not graduate from high school. St. Paul's, FEDSEM, and St. Bedes qualified candidates with unaccredited Licentiate Certificates and

Diplomas. Reputable educational institutions such as the Universities of Natal and Rhodes, across the street from Anglican seminaries, did not recognize these certificates for ongoing study. Only the FEDSEM offered the Associateship, which qualified students for the Bachelor of Arts (Honours) program at Natal University. Only a tiny, select few seized this opportunity. Not many after ordination pursued study to address the need for education in the modern world.

The need for a reasonable basis of education declined further in the 80s. ESSA opened its doors in Pietermaritzburg, South Africa. This institution prided itself on its American conservative evangelical ideologies, creating programs for church ministry for students who had not graduated from high school. Evangelicalism prides itself on the literal "reading" of the Bible, conservative values, and fear of thought outside the cave in the USA. Evangelicals' fundamentalist beliefs include the literal existence of a fantastic alternative universe, disbelief in the new Science, and critical thinking. Others seminarians in Southern Africa pursued remote learning through the Church's internal Theological Education by Extension program. Others completed some courses with UNISA. As the Charismatic Renewal seized complete control, the Church selected candidates for the new order of "community priests." These candidates qualified on the strength of solid pastoral gifts such as praying, preaching, and leading worship, with very little academic training. The push to ordain candidates for the order of "eucharistizers" – sacrament consecraters- to preside over communion services did not go far.

The Renewal or Charismatic Movement's idea of "body ministry" and "Holy Spirit Experience " arrogance vigorously and successfully protested anti-intellectualism and won. Thus, the fourth leg of "subjective experience" supplanted the traditional three-legged stool of the ancient Anglican wisdom tradition.

The Charismatic Renewal raised many unqualified, lazy, senior, and junior clerics, with solid ministerial gifts for particular local ministries, great talents for worship, and numerical growth. However, talent for moving the Church beyond its numerical development and health needs towards missional activity lies dormant for lack of identification, education, and training. Leaders also lack the talent to model and teach the much-needed relevant holistic spirituality for the contemporary secular world. Untrained clergy leads inward-focused selfish congregations whose business fails to deliver essential service to their restless impoverished local communities and world. The justice before peace ministry in most churches does not enjoy a prominent place in local ministry. Some Liberal activist churches fail to save those trapped in unjust systems and structures. Liberal churches achieve only partial success, lopping leaves and leaving roots, stem, and branches intact.

Honest leadership cannot ignore or deny real needs in the immediate neighborhood, national state, and world. Unfortunately, most local churches' response to social needs and unrest is not on the long-term plan or the usual monthly meeting. There may be a mission plan but no missional strategy. Since the Charismatic movement, churches have spent much energy planning the next exciting Sunday worship concert. Bible study programs focus on selfish personal health and success, constantly turning the gaze away from those hurting and hoping in the neighborhood and world. In these churches, the Holy Spirit of Truth is seldom allowed to lead to the fullness of Truth. Literalism, the un- Anglican reading approach to the Christian scriptures, has become widely accepted. For the suppression of Truth, gaslighting, deflection, subject-changing, canceling, denial, defense, etc., typically characterize unproductive discourse in the marketplace of religion.

The Church's essential educational qualification in the USA and most parts of the world is a master's post-graduate degree at a fully accredited institution of learning, a certificated course in hospital chaplaincy, mandated ongoing continuing education, sabbaticals for rest, and the procurement of various other academic and professional skills for ministry. In apartheid South Africa, only Whites qualified with an undergraduate degree with an internship at Seminary. There was a time when all the senior leaders came from the Caucasian group. The American Dioceses required that clergy regularly retreat for education, spirituality, and orientations in practical ministry. Synods called Annual Conferences in the USA focus beyond its usual law revision and lawmaking business, making time for mini training seminars for the clergy and lay.

The Anglican Church globally was an organization that depended solely on wealthy benefactors. The metropolitan Church in the USA comprises a small strong church, the majority belonging to the poor precariat. In SA, Black churches are enormous due to biological growth but poor. In poverty, especially in urban America, the wise local Church collectively accumulates power by establishing partnerships with others organizing around neighborhood needs. Solid, intelligent, organizational skills for collective action have proved necessary for the health and wealth of the local church community. These partnerships initiate projects that impact the health of the community surrounding the church plant. A good, well-trained leader wakes the local Church to its mandated ministry to its immediate community. Trained core interest groups within the Church, surveyed and identified neighborhood needs for crucial programs and projects designed with community involvement. Each local congregation identifies at least one excellent program to make it famous in the local community, the Diocese, and the world.

The dying churches in the USA in deprived, disinvested urban and rural neighborhoods thrive on collaborative partnerships. They provide low-income housing, day-care facilities, food pantries, soup kitchens, meeting places, etc., for the community. On the south side of Chicago, Trinity Church and St. Edmund's survived death because they formed strong self-interest liaisons for successful collective projects and programs. Community organizing skills make solid leaders for the local Church and society. At Trinity Church in Chicago, successful partnerships in the neighborhood raised enough money to free its poor congregation from the burden of tithing what little money they earned. Instead, members were encouraged to use their tithing money for personal generosity programs for needy folk in the neighborhood. St. Edmund's Church still expects the small, mainly middle-class community to drop something into the collection plate to inflate its savings account. Recently St. Edmund's Church received $1 million from its Community Housing Project that provides low-income affordable housing.

The Diocese of Chicago, facing a money crisis, took inventory of its property assets and identified money-making projects for missional projects and developmental needs in local parishes. The Methodists in downtown Durban did the same many years ago. A long time ago, the Diocese of Natal allowed the whites at St. Paul's, Durban, to build the Ogwini Apartments, which translated into cash for St. Paul's and the Diocese. St. Paul's, Pietermaritzburg, sold Esther Payne's school property for R 200,000, a paltry sum in 1984. St. Paul's and Holy Angels, Pietermaritzburg could have made more if the Diocese saw fit to partner with these two churches to venture with the developer jointly. St. John's, Pinetown, made some money off its day-care project. In these last days of the Diocese of Natal, an inventory of Diocesan assets for creative usage to build wealth for the Diocese of parishes and missions is crucial. The Diocese needs leadership to manage property for good stewardship of its solid assets. It cannot depend on the old-fashioned stewardship method alone to raise money for burgeoning and much-needed mandated missional activity. The people are many but poor.

Regular processions around altars, leaders dressed in red-tasseled birettas, red-ribbed costumes, swinging smelly pots, dancing, and shouting alleluias does not do successful ministry. Influential, effective leaders do the necessary for a thriving parochial church. They shovel shit off the filthy streets, feed, educate, clothe the poor, and march for justice in protest in solidarity with the paranoid, hysterical populous to protest the reasons for social unrest. Organizing leadership means time away from the office desk, keeping alert and socially active in a dysfunctional neighborhood, city, state, nation, and global, pluralist world. Success depends on non-judgmental egalitarian partnerships with others in the ashram, synagogue, and mosque. Praying with arms raised for God to descend must be balanced with dancing feet alongside God present in others, dancing in solidarity with hurting and hoping partners.

Good leaders walk in God's spirit, live in liminal space, the kingdom of God. Dysfunctional public behavior signals a misguided spirituality, the loss of control of compulsions of the physical body, and the egoist mind divorced from God. This condition affects all types of spiritual, religious persons- the traditional, charismatic-sanctified, or activist. *All sin and fall short of the glory of God the Christ.* In the USA, tongue-speaking Evangelicals kill Palestinians. Traditional-minded Catholics cross themselves before marching to kill Hispanics in Latin America. Veteran social activists now deplete the coffers of the South African government. Other activists, measured against human standards, have been rewarded with jobs in other countries, higher clerical orders, stained windows in churches, high State or church jobs, statues, etc. All their work has not produced much except more corruption. Archbishop Desmond Tutu quoted the phrase coined by Jean-Baptiste Alphonse in 1849: *The more things change, the more they remain the same.*

The three often used spiritualities- traditional, charismatic-sanctified, and activist-fail to significantly change corrupt world leaders and world orders. The ancient yogic tradition of the mystic Jesus of Nazareth is the corrective to the three spiritualities- traditional, sanctified, and activist. Paul, also a mystic, gently reminded his tongue-speaking

Church to walk in love and the fruits of God's spirit. The fruits, pieces of God, manifest as love, joy, peace, gentleness, kindness, etc., signaled connection with the true inner self, the Christ in all. Jesus provided the key to his spirituality- discipleship or learning, the kenosis or dissolving the Ego, union with God in creation, availability to God's grace for personal transformation, and partnership with God's missional activity in the world. Paul also taught that fleshly compulsive dysfunctions are hatred, discord, jealousy, fits of rage, selfish ambition, dissensions, party intrigues (tribalism), and envy. These toxic symptoms signal divorce from one's physical and spiritual body and an unspiritual life which destroys solidarity or ubuntu with God, neighbor, other creatures, and the planet.

Both traditional, charismatic enthusiasts and religious activists succumb to the compulsions of the spiritually lazy physical body and idle mind. Laziness results from not living in union with the universal Christ incarnate in all creation. The modern era demands a spirituality based on understanding the tri-partite physical structure of humans as body, mind, and spirit. The success of living the Jesus -gospel depended on the loss or death of the Ego. Jesus's spirituality embraced extreme physical and mental practices aimed at disciplining the body and the mind. He believed in scientific facts and constantly talked about the sky, birds, nests, lilies, the water, etc. He followed a lifestyle of contemplative prayer in the kingdom of God, known in the mystic tradition as the liminal space, the dark place of waiting patiently for the God of the Dawn. The mind and the physical body- are the outer shell- one's selfish self-made body centered on establishing public persona measured against other humans. The third body, Christ's spirit, is one's true self made in the image and likeness of God. In the life before death, humans must strive to live into the true self, Christ. The standard of measurement in God's kingdom is nothing else than the perfection of

Christ's unconditional love for others. Humans, to be leaders, seek to attain a higher consciousness by living into the fullness of Christ.

The present age demands contemplative religion, accompanied by awareness, mindfulness, and solidarity with others. The godly leader encounters God in all creation. Successfully practicing awareness means an ever-expanding library of relatively new books and global fellowship. In this Information Age, wisdom and unconditional love knowledge are easily accessible through the God-provided worldwide Web. Mindfulness spurs the heart for a compassionate and empathetic response to neighbors, friends, enemies, and strangers alike.

The modern leader in a fast-paced, rapidly changing world must be Renaissance. The leader must strive to be well-rounded, multi-disciplined, multi-talented, an avid learner, a listener, and a perpetual student with an open inquiring mind. The alert leader today is bombarded with knowledge and wisdom at the speed of nanoseconds constantly. The only qualification needed in the Age of Information is living the words: *I don't know.* No single leader can deliver effectively. Consultative leadership styles and the practice of solidarity with others are essential. What is impossible for one is possible with God in the many. A Great leader- teacher always defers to the greatness in others. Humility recognizes that ordination does not come with the fantastic blessing of everything needed for ministry. Ordination merely sets one on the student's pilgrim path with the gift of the universal Christ to practice awareness, mindfulness, and solidarity.

Maslow's Hierarchy of Needs, its highest level for the abundant, fulfilled life, ubuntu, relational living, synergistic action- must be the beacon, the guiding goal. As one climbs the ladder of hierarchical needs, one practices discipleship, letting go of the excessive compulsions of the physical body and mind. According to James Fowler, the religious must forgo infantile faith and reach the highest level of universal spirituality to navigate life in a pluralist age.

Every institution changes every 500 years. It has been more than 500 years since the Great Reformation. At the turn of his civilization's era, Jesus recommended a complete overhaul of the religious institution. He called for *New wineskins for the new wine.* Wineskins are a direct reference to leaders in the institution, and the wine is God's spirit, the universal Christ. New or renewed educated leaders will lead with enlightened learning for wise, practical pastoral ministry and contemplative wisdom spirituality grounded in oneness with the God within creation. In this dark period of uncertainty, may the God of the Dawn enlighten a new path of love, care, and concern for others and the planet on which we live.

NINETEEN

At the end of an era, things fall apart, especially Ego's vain creations.
The religious try desperately to make sense of the collapse of civilization,
its institutions, systems, and structures. Distress, depression, and anxiety
trouble the human heart amidst widespread social unrest and destruction.
Questions abound in the marketplace of discourse. Is God destroying evil?
Or is God revealing something new for fresh starts and a better future?

Eschatological Apocalypse

The Bible accurately describes the present time as the last days of a passing era, the sunset of a jaded civilization. The appropriate description for such a universal moment of uncertainty and calamity in history is an apocalypse. Historians note that cultures and institutions routinely change every 500 years. The decline of Ego's world of division, deprivation, social unrest, paranoia, hysteria, and depression affects the soul and tired body. Yet, times of trouble are also times of hope. From the black darkness of the coal yard heap, hope in the form of a lily always springs eternal.

Some breathe a deep sigh of relief. Decay and destruction are sure signs that the old order of evil is giving way to the new. Wide-eyed prophets emerge from the dark wilderness, the place of shadows into the daylight speaking in misunderstood tones of doom, gloom, and themes of "end times." Awakened others privately know that the word "apocalypse" means "revelation." They speak with authority that God bursts forth from the darkness of death, revealing the wisdom of the new way at the crossroads, a time of jubilee and restoration. For the hopeful-wise, unlike the "doom and gloom" group, the word "apocalypse" cannot be associated with the word "eschatology," which suggests the "end times" and destruction. Where there is God, there is life. God, like the potter, always picks up the broken pieces, molds new shapes carefully with loving hands, breathing new life into new forms. God is able and does this on grander scales, like shifting continental shelves under the oceans. In moments when continents and civilizations topple and disappear into the ocean or desert sand, God breathes spirit into water and dust. God reorders and recreates emerging forms of fauna and flora for a new world within the destruction. As in Hegel's dialectic thought, God's pattern follows *thesis, antithesis, and synthesis.* Richard Rohr of the Center of Action and Contemplation translates this as *order, disorder, and reorder.*

In times of trouble, the soul seeks its true inner self through the practice of contemplation. But first, the soul discards its old baggage, its physical and mental accumulations - the egoist world of shadows. Humans spend much time in the shadows, devoting enormous energy and space to the tyranny of physical compulsions and mental desires. The Ego, desirous of independence, foregoes innocence and separates itself from its true inner self where God's spirit of essential love, grace, and compassion abounds. Unlike the esoteric doomsayers who believe Ego's illusion of God living socially distant from humans and the world, the "awoke" contemplatives in the wisdom tradition encounter God within the true self and creation. Those in touch with their true selves speak of the close God. Muslims believe that God is as close as the jugular vein. Christians call God Immanuel, the God with humans. The near God, ever-present, does not destroy but re-members, making whole the world's brokenness and individual lives. God presides over a global eucharist service when the world falls apart, putting together carefully the fractured parts of lives and the world.

A significant part of Christendom awaits Parousia, the second coming of a destructive Jesus. Did Jesus, the Christ-incarnate word of God, come to partner in God's apocalyptic destruction of the world? Or did Jesus come to reveal to humankind God's way of love, healing, wholeness, return, redemption, reformation, and transformation at the end of a historical era? What do the gospels say?

The synoptic gospels are cultural gospels constructed for an apology and evangelistic conversion of others. They portray a tribal Jesus standing above tribal culture and not compassionately sensitive to other cultures. Mark "apologized" the Christian way to Gentiles, Matthew to Jews and Luke and Paul to Greeks and Romans entangled in mysterious, parallel, pagan, philosophical religions. These falsely-named gospel evangelists portrayed Jesus as an apocalyptic preacher bringing doom and gloom to other cultures, religions, and beliefs. No wonder missionaries assumed the missionary position when telling the story to global pagans. Unfortunately, many evangelists continue the practice with the same aloof, bigotrous attitudes. Evangelists in Christendom preach theology that includes belief in Jesus, an apocalyptic-eschatological emissary sent by a distant, angry God of punishment and destruction.

Luke and Paul pursued a slightly diplomatic and different approach when speaking to others. They followed the mystic wisdom tradition. Paul demonstrated this understanding approach in his sermon at the Areopagus. Luke and Paul began with the goodness of God already present in those they visited. Their theological starting point was the presence of the universal God in all tribal religious cultures. The Lucan-Paul message preached the God who is apocalyptic-revelatory. God presents with revelation (apocalypse) in personal trauma and global crisis (eschatology) with grace for empowerment.

John, the evangelist, operated wholly within the mystic wisdom tradition. On the scale of *Fowler's Stages of Faith*, John's faith surpassed the infantile stage of fearful religion that promoted judgment, spiritual and social apartheid on others. John's mature faith acknowledged the God of creation incarnate in all creation, loving, restoring, and healing. In John's gospel, God poured down rain on the just and the unjust and was OK with life's contradictions. John's Jesus was not an apocalyptic preacher, arriving at the close of an era to preach the end of all things evil. For John, God's spirit, the Christ, came to reveal God's way of unconditional love for all. Humans in Christ can participate in Christ's mission of love by lending the human physical body and mind to Christ. St. Teresa of Avila observed that Christ, who is spirit, has no physical body except ours.

Christ has no body but yours,
No hands, no feet on earth but yours,
Yours are the eyes with which Christ looks
Compassion on this world,
Yours are the feet with which Christ walks to do good,
Yours are the hands with which Christ blesses all the world.
Yours are the hands, yours are the feet,
Yours are the eyes, you are Christ's body.
Christ has no body now but yours,
No hands, no feet on earth but yours,
Yours are the eyes with which Christ looks
compassion on this world.
Christ has no body now on earth but yours.

—

The critical mystic wisdom tradition dispels the belief that any future descent of God spells the end of the planet or the Cosmos. God created with Godself. Any destruction of the Cosmos or the planets would also mean the destruction of God. God cannot descend from elsewhere, for God's name is Emmanuel, God with us. God never leaves or forsakes.

The "end of the world" simply means the end of an era and the arrival of a new future. Jesus preached the kingdom of God within, the realized fateful place of those saved from the false self, the Ego. Awareness of God's presence in the shadows of the physical body and mind means the end of the Ego and the arrival of the evolutionary new human for the changing world. Therefore, the morbid eschatological phrase of the "end of the world" cannot be accurate and true.

The definition of "true" is that which is eternal. Only God is infinite, not fleeting or temporal. God's creation is in part spirit, the substance of God's essence that is incorruptible, eternal, everlasting. In creation, only the physical body, made from the dust of the earth, is temporary, corrupt, and mortal. Paul assures us that the old physical will be exchanged for a more resilient form to accommodate the change. The mind, an essential part of the dusty physical body, is also physically perishable. Ego's mental creations are an illusion, a lie, corruptible, fleeting, prone to decay. Only that what God creates with God's essence is eternal, truth, and sound. At death, God's unconditional love replaces Ego's division and privation. Death, Sin, the separation of God, civilization, human institutions are illusionary mental creations of the Ego. The passage of time proves their temporality and unreality.

The eschatological judgment of permanent death and final destruction implied in the terms "last days" cannot refer to the more significant part of the Cosmos comprised of God's eternal spirit, the universal Christ. The same in part applies to all humans, other living creatures, and the planet made in the image and likeness of God. That which is of God in creation cannot die. For mystics in the wisdom tradition, the term "last days" can only mean the end of the reign of Ego and its mental creations that sustain division, deprivation, social unrest, and the corrupt human condition. Also, for contemplative mystics, "apocalypse" is the moment of God's new revelation for a new future. Therefore, the mystic heart of hope always springs eternal. God is present amidst Ego's disappearing illusions of death, destruction, and social dysfunction. Habakkuk, a minor prophet, prayed in troubled times, patiently waiting for the dawn of a new era. The central theme of his book is the triumph of the human spirit, growing from a faith of perplexity and doubt to cruise at the mature height of absolute trust in God.

Although the fig tree shall not blossom, neither shall fruit be in the vines; the labor of the olive shall fail, and the fields shall yield no meat; the flock cut off from the fold, and there shall be no herd in the stalls: Yet I will rejoice in the Lord. I will joy in the God of my salvation.

Paul, the mystic, wrote to the suffering church in Rome in an apocalyptic era of Empire collapse, assuring them, no matter the circumstance, of God's loving presence.

[35]Who shall separate us from the love of Christ? Shall tribulation, or distress, or persecution, or famine, or nakedness, or peril, or sword? [36]As it is written, For thy sake, we are killed all the day long; we are accounted as sheep for the slaughter. [37]Nay, in all these things, we are more than conquerors through him that loved us. [38]For I am persuaded, that neither death, nor life, nor angels, nor principalities, nor powers, nor things present, nor things to come, [39]Nor height, nor depth, nor any other creature, shall be able to separate us from the love of God, which is in Christ Jesus our Lord.

C.S. Lewis, in an essay in 1948, at the height of the 2nd World War, raised the existential question of the pursuit of life amid a new global crisis. The crisis was the war but more the impending use of the newly invented atomic bomb. In this essay, Lewis advises that people should quietly live as people lived in every other age. Chances of serious disaster continuously abound. He cautioned that people should *not* exaggerate the novelty and gravity of their particular situation. He scolded that it was "perfectly ridiculous to go about whimpering and to draw long faces because scientists have added one more chance of painful and premature death to a world already bristling with such chances, and in which death itself was not a chance at all, but a certainty." He advised what steps one should take when faced with the possibility of death: He goaded: "Pull yourselves together, and if you are going to be destroyed by whatever is going around, let it find you doing sensible things like praying, working, teaching, reading, listening to music, bathing the children, playing tennis, chatting to your friends over a pint and a game of darts- not huddled together like frightened sheep and thinking about impending disasters. He encouraged: "They may break our bodies, but they cannot dominate our minds."

Ken Wilber, a teacher at the *Center of Contemplation and Action*, says that humans possess an inner state and an outer state. The internal state is where God's spirit, the Christ, resides. In times of crisis and trauma, the physical body, the first form of defense, responds instinctively from the outer state, the weaker state. Jesus taught: *Greater is that which is within you than that which is outside of you.* With contemplation, one can live habitually into one's more vital stronger state.

We know that the whole creation is groaning together in the pains of childbirth until this hour. God is bringing into this world God's new creation. God is in the destruction within and surrounding one, the pain and misery of social dysfunction and social unrest, the aborted mental fetuses of rapacious social, political, economic structures, and sacred and secular institutions. Let us not exaggerate the novelty of our present particular situation. Let us not go about paralyzed, whimpering, and drawing long faces that Ego has added to our chances of painful and premature death. Let us, the ordinary, take extraordinary steps when faced with the possibility of death. Let us leave Ego behind, take up the cross of love, and follow the footsteps of Christ in the ways of radical love. Let us do sensible things like praying, working, reading, listening to music, bathing the children, playing tennis, chatting to our friends over a pint and a game of darts. In the words of Mr. Lewis: They may break our bodies, but they cannot break our spirits.

Mystics experience God's spirit, the incarnate Christ in the creation, and the inner self. In the darkness of night, the mystic soul encounters revelation via the God of the apocalypse through the spiritual practice of contemplation. Those who combine "apocalypse" with "eschatology" to mean destruction intensify fear, anxiety, distress, and belief in an egoist concept of absentee God who cannot deliver immediate welfare service. In the present age of faith, the soul's welfare and the redemption of this world hang on the dissolving of two things: The Ego and the concept of God.

TWENTY

The following sermon reflects on the violent social unrest in South Africa because of injustice stemming from inept and corrupt management. The beautiful people of this southern tip of the African continent long for lasting peace based on land reform, equity, respect of dignity, and the solidarity of mutual care, or ubuntu. Since Archbishop Tutu publicized ubuntu to the world, especially in the USA, exceptionalist understanding of a lifestyle has been reduced to a concept. This paper proposes that ubuntu is a universal expression of communal love for transformation deeply embedded in the genes of all humans. All cultural heroes, like Jesus, lived out of ubuntu.

Jesus and Ubuntu

In the week of July 18, 2021, a significant portion of KwaZulu-Natal, and Johannesburg rudely woke to a tsunami of violence to property and people. The port city of Durban and its surrounding townships have been the hardest hit. Unfortunately, the country has not recovered from the shock and awe. The future of the country seems bleak, and relationships between the various national groups remain fragile. One wonders since the regime change and the Covid-19 pandemic, the country battling mismanagement and corruption will ever trace its steps backward on the slippery slope to utter destruction.

Ubuntu – the Zulu/Shona/ Xhosa/ Ndebele/ Sesotho word for *umuntu ngumuntu ngabantu (Zulu)*-translates into Imperial English as *"I am because we are."* The African philosophy of *ubuntu* emphasizes achieving self-meaning through others without an external deity's influence. Many, both secular and religious, raise the standard of *ubuntu* as the social solution to the present violence in South Africa. However, *ubuntu,* more a way of life than a conceptual standard, has failed. In its purest form in Africa, *ubuntu* is humanist, leaving God out of the influence equation on individuals for communal living. The recent incidents of violence in Natal and the city of Gauteng prove what happens in exceptionalist, egoist, humanist communities without the knowledge of God under the oppressive control of powerful charismatic leadership. *Ubuntu,* popularized globally by Archbishop Desmond Tutu in a speech and lectures in the USA, has degraded to a nationalist belief or great idea. What was a way of life, still a socialist practice in the poor village, is almost totally absent in urban and suburbia hearts. The recent events of looting, violence, and insurrection are cases in point.

Nevertheless, the concept still lives large in the minds of the middle class and those in academia. They say that the longest road to travel is between the head to the heart. Thus, for example, a wealthy CEO of Ubuntu Wealth Management looted large appliances in the recent riots.

The lifestyle or concept of *ubuntu* is a universal, transnational, global phenomenon, as explained below. But, sadly, those resistant to knowledge in the present Information Age, stubborn to scientific facts, pride themselves on an exceptionalist understanding of *ubuntu.* Maslow gifted the West the conceptual structure of self-understanding, namely the *Hierarchy of Needs.* He believed that attaining *ubuntu,* the highest hierarchical level of need for solidarity with others, is impossible among humans. On the other hand, those in the Orient and Abrahamic religions know that *ubuntu* is attainable because of the universal spirit within the soul. Jesus and Paul of the Abrahamic tradition recognized the absence of the universal energy in the late Jewish legalistic religion. Nevertheless, they found that the Oriental form of *ubuntu- ubuntu* with God- was still alive in the suppressed mystic tradition in Judaism. The success of the Jesus and Paul movements thrived because of the experience of *ubuntu* in Christ, God's spirit.

Hysterical scramblers have instantly responded with simple solutions in the recent wave of violence to self, property, and others in South Africa. Some prayed, blazoned flags on landmarks, shared kumbaya lyrics on social media, and bonded to clean up businesses and streets. Some claim that these civic and religious actions are the perfect expression of *ubuntu*. Raising standards appeal to a small group easily guilted and shamed and offers no sustainable solution. However, these human acts do provide temporary comfort provincially and regionally. The Jesus of John's gospel desires a perfect expression of *ubuntu,* the global movement of love for joy based on oneness with the God within, with hope for national and international *ubuntu- one world, one God, one people.*

Today, we possess 20/20 hindsight. Human history records human failures. The garbage dumps fill and destroy our landscapes with failed systems and structures, fundamentalist religion, institutional religion, theologies (North-Western and Liberation), religious movements, ideologies, philosophies, etc. Activists for liberation in South Africa acknowledge their grand mistake of setting the stage for self-centered, self-serving, greedy, corrupt winners. Some still cling to failed secular and religious liberation ideologies. In Natal and Western Cape, exceptionalist cultural communities gather, using failed theologies to inform and educate. Globally, the phenomenon of nationalism, apartheid/ exceptional *ubuntu,* is on the rise. Historians today are aware of the failure of past humanistic social and intellectual endeavors. Like Jesus, historians comment that the apparent failure is the *kairos* moment for critical change for solidarity, social justice, and spiritual experience.

Three million years of study in primate behavior concludes the size of the brain has much to do with the loss of *ubuntu*. The human brain has tripled in size over 3 million years to fill its 2.5 lb. mass in the human skull. Most of its growth happened in the last 2 million years. The significant brain saw the rise of personal and communal behavior change. Behavioral scientists observed that primates with smaller brains naturally lived in solidarity to preserve the community.

On the other hand, primates with fully developed brains lived competitively with others. Thus, the philosophy of *ubuntu* existed without exceptionalism, division, and deprivation of others at one stage of the evolutionary development of the human species. However, the large brain size heralded ego-consciousness. With the rise of ego-consciousness came the loss of oneness in God and socialist spirit-relational living for collaborative care.

Jesus, who practiced discernment of the loss of relationship with God and socialism in humans, noticed the presence of Ego by its conscious disposition to self-service without regard for others. The philosophy of relational, synergistic, communal living is not just the private possession of Africans. In the West, Maslow's highest hierarchical need resembles the need for fulfillment through the community. In Oriental philosophy, Confucius proposed the Golden Rule- love your neighbor as you love yourself. The Abrahamic religious tradition, the people of the Book, Jews, Christians, and Muslims, raise the standard of *ubuntu* for the community's survival.

The Eastern and Western Judaeo- Christian- Islamic traditions differ from the extreme humanist understanding of *ubuntu* in the African philosophy. God as the indwelling universal spirit (Christ in the Christian tradition) blesses and guides the course of ubuntu in the community. Jesus was acutely aware of the human failure of his times- pious spiritual movements, political liberation movements, identity theologies, and exceptionalist failed fundamentalist and orthodox religions. Moreover, he lived in one of the outposts of the declining Roman Empire. Jesus, the man, possessed more wisdom than knowledge. He identified the only primary flaw in social dysfunction was the presence of Ego in humans. For Jesus, humans could never be humans outside of the God within. Unfortunately, Ego convinces humans that God embraced dualist philosophy. As a result, humans suffer the loss of memory of who they are in God- wonderfully made of God's essence in God's *image and likeness. So* Jesus proposed a practical gospel that he lived: *If anyone wishes to be a follower, let that person leave self (Ego) behind, take up the cross [of love], daily and follow me.*

Because of the presence of the Ego, *ubuntu* is not a birthright, a natural inclination, an entitlement of racial ethnicity, a private national possession. On the contrary, *ubuntu,* the primordial learned behavior of unconditional love, the nature of the human soul, though a natural lifestyle, waits patiently in the shadows of liminality. The soul awaits resurrection by sacrificing the false self, the Ego, and the graceful power for a new way of being in this world. *Ubuntu is* a way of life only powered by the presence of God within.

Jesus's gospel proposed no failed belief, philosophy, theology, ideology. Nor did he offer failed human systems and structures that produce corrupt leaders, violent and corrupt fractured societies. Instead, Jesus submitted *ubuntu* as the perfect solution with one caveat- *in Christ,* the universal Christ, the spirit of God. Thus, *ubuntu* is the lifestyle for those in the Kingdom of God. Let the Kingdom of God reign in the soul and the land.

Globally there is a rising tide of patriotism and national pride, which contributes to *exceptionalist ubuntu.* This phenomenon is encouraged and used by corporate capitalism, which thrives on the large-scale policy of divide and rule. At the colonial outposts, majority rule persists.

Despised minority groups, in search of power, justice, and dignity, make a plausible case for exceptionalist ubuntu. Nonetheless, in a world the size of a global village, the argument for universal *ubuntu* is more reasonable.

The church, those called into *ubuntu* living, still has only the Jesus gospel to proclaim, especially in the cradle of *ubuntu*. Therefore, *if one wishes to be a follower of God, practice spirituality daily, live in God, leave Ego behind, be a learner/ disciple, and live ubuntu intentionally.* This gospel truth of Jesus of Nazareth is still relevant. Therefore, the Huddleston Prayer for Africa must undergo a minor revision in corrupt Africa:

> *Nkosi Sikelel' iAfrika (God bless Africa) Guide, her leaders,*
> *Guard her children And give her justice before peace*

TWENTY-ONE

*Two thousand years of philosophical tradition has played down
direct, close encounters with the universal Christ in creation.
The dominant theological illusion of God separating from the
world poses problems for the spiritual path of self-understanding,
transformation, moral conscience, and honest relationships.
Nevertheless, inherent coercive love still propels one to embrace one's
true self, the essence of God's moral conscience and purpose.*

The Christ, Consciousness, and Conscience

Magicians never give up the secrets of their trade. Likewise, shamans, gurus, and ministers, to preserve their mystique, behave like inscrutable magicians. Among the clergy, the goal of mystery facilitates dominant transcendental leadership styles. Jesus, the man from Galilee, never flaunted an aura of mystery surrounding his persona, ministry, and successful life. On the contrary, he was transparent, open, free, graceful, and generously gave away all that he gracefully learned and acquired from God in liminal space. Jesus, like God, did not discriminate, raining blessings on the righteous and unrighteous.

Jesus practiced oneness or solidarity with all, especially his tiny core community of learners. This oneness translated into healthy, respectful, powerful relationships. As a mendicant, highly respected mystical leader, Jesus enjoyed a unique, unusual, and equitable relationship with his followers. Yet, he assured them in a culturally, imperial, exploitative, capitalist context:

I no longer call you slaves because a slave does not know his master's business. Instead, I have called you friends, for I have made known everything that I learned from my Father.

Jesus lightened the darkness of life's shadows, shining the bright light of love for gracious living with others. As a wonder- worker, he practiced his vocation without needing Ego's false mystique for control by fear.

Jesus felt secure enough to give away the deepest secrets of successful living to whomsoever. He had learned to curb the base desires of greed, hoarding, longing, and belonging. Jesus lived his life off the grid of grift. So, he would have agreed with the following wisdom on the verse of Psalm 23:

The Lord is my Shepherd. Therefore, I do not need anything.

Jesus, the human embodiment of the divine, found it impossible to hold onto anything material: his religion, spirituality, profound cognitive or intuitive knowledge of God, talents, and practical wisdom. Tradition, especially the conflicting records of the canonical writings, has buried his wise message for fulfilled, significant living. As a result, the gospel of Jesus remains a well-kept secret, awaiting only the questioning learner who practices awareness in this world.

Jesus's way of truth for life stands on the solid foundation of contemplation and action that emanated from the existential encounter with Christ in creation. Spiritual practices sustained this relationship with the Christ- the dissolution of the Ego, contemplative alertness or consciousness, openness to personal transformation into beings of conscience, and solidarity with others for just and fair relationships. The man from

Nazareth grounded his life in God's unconditional love, the solitary moral principle in the universe.

Traditional Christianity during the Great Councils of debating the persona of Jesus, and the 19th Century American Protestant Reformations, erred by fixating on the man Jesus of Nazareth- especially his death and resurrection for the believer's salvation. The result was that Jesus the man became God, assuming the work of God's spirit, the Christ. This conciliar exercise of making the man Jesus God was written in stone by the 19th Century American Protestant church's reform work. The reform work ignored God's historical, continual, creating, loving, saving relationship with humanity that began long before the birth of the historical Jesus two thousand years ago.

The Christ, the essential loving God, existed at the creation, infused everything, and has been present in all cultures and civilizations. Emmanuel, a name for God, is the One who never leaves or forsakes creation. However, the man Jesus, a historical embodiment of God's spirit, the Christ, is the best example of accessing God's heart of love. Today, no one can approach God's love except through the example of the embodied Christ in Jesus of Nazareth. But God, as the Cosmic Christ, constantly infuses everything, making everything sacred in the natural world. God the Christ is the messianic savior, always a new revelation in the world, a new incarnation each time a creature is born. Paul, a Jew of the highest order, speaks of this Christ mystery in his letters. Christ, he says, is the indwelling divine presence in everyone, the gift of God when, like Jesus, humans dissolve or crucify the Ego. The mystic John explains that Christ is the light of God, enlightening all born in time and space.

Since the Enlightenment of the seventeenth and eighteenth centuries, the philosophy of dualism drove a wedge between creator and creation, significantly increasing the distance between God and creation. The absence of God created space for Ego to take the stage center in the affairs of humans and the world. After the Western Church separated from the East in the Great Schism in 1054, Westerners lost sensitivity to God's immediate, unmediated, continuous, loving, and saving activity in creation. Nevertheless, great people of God like Gregory of Nyssa, revered in Western and Eastern Christianity, testified that deity is always in everything. Jesus, too, knew of God's closeness. In John's gospel, in the High Priestly Prayer, Jesus prays that all people may be like him- one with the Father. In the words of his biographer Luke, Paul knew of the God in whom one lived, moved, and had existence.

This oneness with God is God's gift at creation for everyone and everything before birth in this world. The Christ within is the glorious secret for the reordering of self and the world. But, unfortunately, since the unfolding of ego-consciousness, humans have been under Ego's oppressive spell of the illusory belief that God is distant and separate from creation. The human mind erroneously believes God is distant, unknowable, or absent from the human condition. Not knowing that one is loved dramatically affects one's perception of others and relationships with others.

Humans and the rest of creation are a cosmos of original goodness and universal relational integrity. God laid the foundations of the world based on the matrix of universal oneness. Therefore, in solving the mistakes of our divisions, oneness must always be the starting point. Meaningful inclusion bases itself on the fact of oneness from the beginning of creation. It has nothing to do with evil, human, social divisions, nation, ethnicity, hierarchies, or allegiances to ideological, political, social, and economic systems and structures. Paul knew this wisdom when dealing with social dysfunction in his wicked, divisive, imperial, exploitative world. He said:

*There is neither Jew nor Greek, male or female,
slave or free, for you are all one in Christ.*

Oneness is not pantheism. Oneness in Christ implies a relationship with divinity in which one's unique identity is preserved and not absorbed into God. Jesus, the man, knew this truth and invested all his energy in his faithful relationship with the incarnate God of spirit. Jesus practiced conscious awareness of the Other in the universe. Oneness with God translated into solidarity, *ubuntu,* community with others, and morality, namely just, fair, and equitable relationships. Jesus knew that the egoist mind of fear, binary and divisive thought without resting, goes around contradicting the practice of oneness with others. Egocentric love cannot love like God, who becomes one with others. Egoist humans seek to serve themselves first, then look towards others for capitalist interests or as mistakes or problems to be solved rather than persons to be loved.

The secret gospel of Jesus - oneness or solidarity with the Christ of love in all things operates fluidly and radically as unconditional love for the community (*ubuntu*) and its healthy social welfare. *Ubuntu* is the Christ in one, recognizing and seeking the Christ of oneness in others and the world. The recognition and seeking constitute the true meaning of faith, contradicting religion's reduction of faith to propositional, conceptual beliefs. Therefore, universally, the essential primary work of all religions is recognizing the divine image in all God's creatures and reflecting this image correctly to others. This image is the secret Paul reveals to all nations in his first letter to the Colossians: *Christ in you, the hope of glory to come.* Thus, there is only one single integrated global community of the Earth connected by one consciousness of Christ, the global mycelium underground matrix of network communication of God's intelligent wisdom of love.

Jesus taught that one could not serve two masters. In his secret gospel, Jesus proposed sacrifice or death of the Ego. This way of life is a spiritual path less traveled in the greedy, consumerist, materialist age. Jesus preached the dissolution of the human Ego and the loss of Ego's worldly creations- civilization- including its sacred and secular institutional systems and structures. He encouraged the *via Dolorosa* -the way of the cross- clearly explained by Paul in his pastoral letter to the Corinthians and Ephesians- firstly, the renunciation of the empty philosophy of dualism and secondly, embracing the life of God's radical, unconditional love. Love is the effective vaccine for the viral dilemma rampant in the dysfunctional world.

The external practice of religion did not sit well with Jesus. He was highly critical of religion, its institutions, and its clergy, who ignored the image of the Christ within. Jesus and Paul, contemplative mystics, followed the spiritual practices of subduing the body to obey its every command. For Jesus, the whole world was a liminal space where darkness, sickness, and death waited patiently for God's Enlightenment. Liminal space is the place of hope, the dynamic end of the small self for the bigger. Ego dissolves when God's light, God's actual image, and likeness appear to dispel the shadows. Knowledge becomes wisdom for the application of truth. Abundant grace empowers the fulfilled life with others. Jesus called liminal space the kingdom of God. Liminal space is where one wastes time in God's presence in creation, prayerfully contemplating the self, others, and the world for meaning and purpose in this world. Jesus looked upon death and life as one phenomenon. St. Francis explained this too in his life:

And it is in dying that we are born to eternal life.

Liminal space is the place of dying and rising for just and fair action in the world.

We live in the geological age known as the Anthropocene epoch. Human activity has been the dominant influence on humanity, climate, and the environment. The visible signs of fever are unmistakable when the Earth is troubled- global warming, rampant wildfires, hurricanes, tornados, and floods. In this era of death and destruction, the Ego and its clever creations- systems, structures, and institutions- sow to the whirlwind, reaping a harvest of death and destruction in its wake. The current mutation of the capitalist system known as necro-capitalism is the harbinger of the end of most of the population shackled as slave-workers in the marketplace. Modern humans are bent on suicide and the destruction of the Earth. In the second World War, man used the atomic bomb to destroy other humans and almost succeeded. The presently preferred instrument of global suicide is the system of capitalism that targets humans and the very ground upon which they stand for its buried wealth.

Humans find it extremely difficult to embrace necessary change. Yet, the difference is essential for a world sliding down a slippery slope to extinction by widespread poverty and loss of joy. Ideology is one of the root causes of decay and death. Nevertheless, there are some lessons to be learned from countries once strangled by ideology. China is a towering prosperous nation proving to the world the success of capitalism in a context of radical social welfare. It has succeeded in lifting a significantly high percentage of its population from the grips of poverty. The reasons for successful change for progress include the rejection of ideology, embracing facts, science, and technology, and opening to the influences in the global market. These principles, which have served the welfare of China, can be the basis for substantial reform in sacred and secular institutions globally. This era is long overdue for the reformation of all human systems, structures, and institutions.

Jesus proposed a way of life that embraced death, but not the kind presented by the selfish Ego. Instead, Jesus grounded his truth and wisdom on the conscious knowledge of one's true nature- the Christ of unconditional love, God's spirit in all. The Christ within is the glorious secret for reordering self and the world based on the sacrifice of the human Ego and radical reform of ego's global and national institutional creations. Jesus encouraged individuals to embrace the life of death in the space we live- this world he named the kingdom of God. This liminal twilight space for contemplation exists for existential perpetual revolution, death, and resurrection. The Anthropocene epoch awaits the birth of the new kind of human, the latest being, conscious of the Christ within. This new human is resolute, strongly purposed to die, and rise with a moral conscience to serve others justice, setting aside the easy option of cheap, liberal peace.

For the present era, the new kind of human is the individual who spends one's life in liminal space asking serious questions about life and goodness. This new being lives conscious of God's *Christian* nature within and without- God's essence of unconditional love- and acts with a moral conscience for the social welfare of all God's people.

ENDNOTES

[i] The Pareto principle is an interesting law that manifests in many contexts. It is also known as "Pareto law", "the law of significant few", "the 80-20 rule". For example: "80% of the land is owned by 20% of the population." https://www.theprojectdefinition.com/pareto-principle-or-80-20-rule/

[ii] Kristopher J. Brooks, *Why so many black businesses professionals are missing from the C-Suite,* https://www.cbsnews.com/news/black-professionals-hold-only-3-percent-of-executive-jobs-1-percent-of-ceo-jobs-at-fortune-500-firms-new-report-says/, December 10, 2019, 9.14am

[iii] Hind Swaraj: Self-Rule of self for self realization and self-rule in India for the wealthy and upper caste.

[iv] The Collect in the Catholic and Anglican/ Episcopal Communion service is an introductory prayer to the s scripture readings for the day.

[v] Ego is not the true self. The true self is the uncreated soul, the image and likeness of God in creation. The sacred scriptures use the words Devil, Lucifer, or Satan to personify Ego's demonic behavior. Jesus, the mystic refers to the false self as the Ego. The true self is the soul, the seat of the God who is love. Biologists refer to the origin of the Ego when brain fully developed became conscious as a separate self producing the illusion of duality. Ego follows decisions linked to past experience, indoctrination, and social forces. Its instinctual drive is connected to programs, and is therefore not self created. The Ego creates an illusion of separation between God and the true self. In these sermons Ego and the Sin as apostasy are intrinsically connected.

vi   Synoptic means from one point of view and different from John's gospel.

vii   Dualism. The philosophical belief that God lives separate from the corrupt world for fear of contamination.

viii   In Genesis, God creates by the speaking the word. In John's prologue, God the logos or Word is the Creator. In Paul's letters, Colossians 1:15-20 and Ephesians 1:3-11, God the universal Christ existed in matter from eternity.

ix   Kingdom of God. An organic contemplative community organized on the principle of God's unconditional love for neighbor in this world.

x   Diaspora. The dispersal of African from the Continent to other parts of the world as slaves.

xi   Satyagraha. The choice of non-violence as a strategy for social, political, and economic change. Its meaning *love force,* is the driving force in the struggle on behalf of the poor, disempowered and voiceless.

REFERENCES

1   Tagore, Rabrindranath, poem *Let My Country Awake,* https://www.goodreads.com/quotes/217931-where-the-mind-is-without-fear-and-the-head-is

2   The word "catholic" means those church's in the Christian tradition that subscribe to the Creeds developed between 325-451 A.D.

3   John 1

4   Colossians 1:17f.

5   Luke 15:7

6   Phillipians 2:1-10. Jesus emptied himself. Theologians used this in what is known as "kenotic theory."

7   Romans 6

8   Rollins, Peter 2008: 138

9   Romans 1:23

10   Rollins 2008:110

11   Harvey Cox:2009:2

12   Otto, Rudolf:1957: xviii

13   Davies:1991:204

14   Davies:1991:204

15   Tippett:2007:2

16   *ibid*

17   *Op cit,p.6*

18   *Op cit, p.2*

19   Harris:2005:67 *also: http://www.youtube.com/watch?v=FHHOiF-dFEg&feature=youtu.be*

20   Tippet:2007:10

21 David Eagleman: http://poptech.org/popcasts/david_eagleman_on_possibilianism

22 I Corinthians 13:2

23 Charles Dickens, Tale of Two Cities, Book 1, p.1

24 Arundhati Roy, Capitalism, A Ghost Story, p. 38

25 http://www.defense.gov/News/Newsarticle.aspx?ID=43313.

26 Galatians 5:22

27 Galatians 5:23

28 Huffington Post, *Has Evangelicalism Become Sociopathic,*

29 Cf. John's gospel prologue

30 I John 3:18,19

31 Romans 13:11

32 https://fondation-frantzfanon.com/interrogating-systemic-racism-and-the-white-academic-field/, Foundation Franz Fanon, June 16, 2020

33 Romans 13:11

34 Romans 12:2

35 Matthew 6:24

36 I Timothy 6:10

37 Proverbs 6:6

38 Romans 8:9

39 John 1:14

40 Ephesians 4: 13

41 2Timothy 3:5

42 Isaiah 40:31

43 Luke 12:49

44 Acts 17:28

45 Galatians 5:22,23

46 Colossians 2:8

47 Ephesians 3:18

48 Galatians 6:14

49 Colossians 1:3-11; Ephesians 1:15-20

50 James 2:14-22

51 Romans 3:10-12, Psalm 53:1-3

52 1John 4:16b-17

53 Romans 8:35-39

54 58:6-8

55 Jeremiah 31:15

56 Galatians 3:28

57 Matthew 26:52

58 CNN International, March 21, 2003

59 Maureen Dowd, " The Xanax Cowboy", *The New York Times*, March 9, 2003, 4, 13.

60 Matthew 5:29

61 James 5:1-6

62 Vandana Shiva, <u>Oneness vs the 10%,</u> vii

63 Revelations 3:16

64 Robet J. Miller (ed.), <u>The Apocalyptic Jesus, A Debate,</u>

65 Phillipians 2:6-8. Theologians used this as a basis of the *kenotic theory,* describing the emptying of God's glory for slave ministry.

66 Amos 5

67 John 3:1-21

68 Colossians 1:16

69 Kester Brewin, <u>Signs of Emergence</u>

70 Joseph R. Myers, <u>Organic Community</u>

71 Federal Theological Seminary of Southern Africa, now closed.

72 Renamed University of KwaZulu Natal, in Durban and Pietermaritzburg

73 ESSA (formerly EBSEMSA). Evangelical Seminary of Southern Africa

74 University of South Africa, based in Pretoria

75 The dawn brings enlightenment in the darkness of trauma, confusion, sickness, death, etc. The Light, the universal Christ is in creation- the Cosmos, leaders, teachers, books, the internet, others,

within, etc. Some name the Dawn by many names. Christians identify the Dawn as the light of the universal Christ renewed educated leaders will lead with enlightened learning for wise, practical pastoral ministry and contemplative wisdom spirituality grounded in oneness with the God within creation. In this dark period of uncertainty, may the God of the Dawn enlighten a new path of love, care, and concern for others and the planet on which we live.

76 Teresa of Avila (1515-1582) (attrib.)

77 Habbakuk 3:17,18

78 Romans 8:

79 John 15:12

80 Galatians 2:20, Colossians 1:27

81 John 1:9

82 Acts 17:28

83 Galatians 3:28

84 I Colossians 1:27b.

BIBLIOGRAPHY

Ambedkar, B.R. & Roy, Arundhati, (2004), *Annihilation of Caste & The Doctor and the Saint,* Brooklyn, New York, Verso.

Armstrong, Karen (1993), *The History of God,* New York, Random House.

Barr, J. (1981). *The Scope and Authority of the Bible.* Philadelphia: Westminister Press.

Bass, D. B. (2012). *Christianity After Religion.* New York, New York: Harper Collins.

Brewin, Kester (2007). *Signs of Emergence,* Grand Rapids, Michigan: Baker Publishing Group.

Brooks, Michael (2020), *Against The Web,* Alresford, Hampshire, John Hunt Publishing.

Brueggemann, W. (2012, May 16). "Jeremiah: Pain and Promise," *The Christian Century,* Chicago

Chomsky Noam (2017), *Requiem for the American Dream,* New York, Seven Stories Press.

Cox, H. (2009). *The Future of Faith.* New York, New York: Harper Collins.

Cronje, Frans (2020), *The Rise or Fall of South Africa,* Heerengracht, Cape Town, Tafelberg

Cupitt, Don (1979), *Jesus and the Gospel,* Chatham, England, W&J Mackay Ltd.

Cupitt, Don (1984), *The Sea of Faith,* Rugby, Warwickshire, Jolly and Barber Ltd.

David Eagleman: http://poptech.org/popcasts/david_eagleman_on_possibilianism

Davies, O. (1991). *Meister Eckhart, Mystic Theologian.* SPCK: London.

De Grasse Tyson, Neil (2017), *Astrophysics for People in a Hurry,* New York, New York, W.W. Norton & Company, Inc.

Douglas Kelly Brown (2015), *Stand your Ground,* Maryknoll, New York, Orbis Books.

Ehrman Bart D. (2014), *How Jesus became God,* New York, New York, Harper Collins.

Ehrman Bart D. (2016), *Jesus Before the Gospels,* New York, New York, Harper Collins.

Flew, Antony, *Stephen Hawking and the Mind of God,* 1996, http://www.infidels.org/library/modern/antony_flew/hawking.html

Fowler, James W (1981), *Stages of Faith, The Psychology of Human Development and Quest for Meaning,* New York, New York, Harper Collins.

Giridharadas, Anand (), (2020), *Winners Take All,* Alfred A. Knoff, New York, Penguin Random House

Harris, S. (2005). *The End of Faith, Religion, Terror and the Future of Reason.* New York: W.W. Norton.

Harris, Sam (2014), *Waking Up,* New York, New York: Simon and Schuster.

Harris, Sam: *http://www.youtube.com/watch?v=FHHOiF-dFEg&feature= youtu.be*

Harvey, V. A. (1981). *The Historian and the Believer.* Philadelphia: The Westminister Press.

Hawkins, David (2013), *Dissolving the Ego,* USA, Hay House.

Hoggan, James (2016), *I'm Right and You're an Idiot,* Gabriola, Canada, New Society Publishers.

Jones, Tony (2015), *Did God Kill Jesus,* New York, New York, Harper Collins.

Myers, Joseph R. (2007), *Organic Community*, Grand Rapids, Michigan: Baker Publishing Group.

Otto, R. (1957). *The Idea of the Holy.* New York, New YorK: Oxford University Press.

Regele, Mike (1995), *Death of the Church,* Grand Rapids, Michigan: Percept Group, Inc.

Rollins, P. (2008). *The Fidelity of Betrayal, Towards a Church Beyond Belief,* Brewster, Massachusetts: Paraclete Press

Rollins, Peter (2009), *The Orthodox Heretic,* Brewster, MA, Paraclete Press.

Roy, Arundhati (2014), *Capitalism,* Chicago, IL, Haymarket Books.

Roy, Arundhati (2016), *The End of Imagination,* Chicago, IL, Haymarket Books.

Roy, Arundhati (2020), *Azad. Freedom. Fascism. Fiction.,* Chicago, IL, Haymarket Books.

Russell, Alec (2009), *After Mandela,* Great Britain: Hutchinson.

Spong, J. S. (1991). *Rescuing the Bible from Fundamentalism*. New York, New York: Harper Collins.

Tickle, P. (2008). *The Great Emergence*. Grand Rapids, Michigan: Baker Publishing Group.

Tippett, K. (2007). *Speaking of Faith*. London: Penguin Books.

Tracy, D. (1981). *The Analogical Imagination, Christian Culture and the Culture of Pluralism*. New York, New York: Crossroad.

Vandana Shiva (2020), *Oneness vs the 1%*, Vermont, USA, Chelsea Green Publishing.

Venter, Lester (1997), *When Mandela Goes*, Great Britain: Mackays of Chatham.

Wilkerson, Isabel (2020), *Caste, The Origins of our Discontents*, New York, Penguin Random House LLC.

Zizek Slavoj (2006), *How to read Lacan*, New York, New York, W.W. Norton & Company Ltd.

Zizek, Slavoj (2020), *A Left Dares to Speak Its Name*, Cambridge, UK, Polity Press.

INDEX

www.ingramcontent.com/pod-product-compliance
Lightning Source LLC
Chambersburg PA
CBHW072126300726
48975CB00003B/947

* 9 7 9 8 8 9 3 5 6 5 9 7 3 *